MORE LAKE DISTRICT

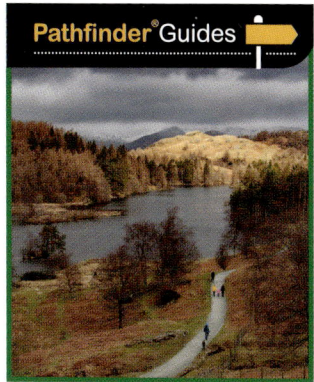

Pathfinder® Guides

Outstanding Circular Walks

Revised by
Vivienne Crow

Contents

At-a-glance

Walk		Page	🖌		🏁	⛰	🕐
1	Great Mell Fell	10	Matterdale End	NY 407 247	2 miles (3.5km)	855ft (260m)	1½ hrs
2	Dalegarth and Eskdale	12	Dalegarth	NY 172 003	3 miles (5km)	280ft (85m)	1½ hrs
3	Rannerdale Knotts	14	Buttermere village	NY 172 172	3 miles (4.5km)	1,015ft (310m)	2 hrs
4	Side Pike and Lingmoor Fell	16	Blea Tarn	NY 296 043	2¾ miles (4.4km)	1,005ft (305m)	2 hrs
5	Aira Force and Gowbarrow Park	18	Patterdale	NY 401 201	4 miles (6.5km)	1,250ft (380m)	2½ hrs
6	Shap Abbey	20	Shap	NY 563 151	4½ miles (7.5km)	425ft (130m)	2 hrs
7	Adam Seat and Harter Fell	24	Mardale Head	NY 469 107	4½ miles (7.2km)	1,755ft (535m)	3 hrs
8	High Rigg and St John's in the Vale	26	Legburthwaite	NY 318 195	5 miles (8km)	1,215ft (370m)	3 hrs
9	Castle Crag and the Jaws of Borrowdale	29	Seatoller	NY 246 138	5 miles (8km)	820ft (250m)	3 hrs
10	Rydal Water and Grasmere	32	Grasmere	NY 339 073	5¼ miles (8.5km)	720ft (220m)	2¾ hrs
11	Glenridding and Lanty's Tarn	35	Glenridding	NY 386 169	5¼ miles (8.5km)	1,015ft (310m)	3 hrs
12	Pavey Ark and Harrison Stickle	38	Great Langdale	NY 294 064	4 miles (6.3km)	2,300ft (700m)	3 hrs
13	Dodd	40	Mirehouse (Dodd Wood)	NY 235 281	4¾ miles (7.5km)	1,740ft (530m)	3 hrs
14	Greendale Tarn, Seatallan and Middle Fell	42	Greendale	NY 144 056	5 miles (8km)	2,460ft (750m)	3½ hrs
15	Bowscale Fell	44	Mungrisdale	NY 364 302	5 miles (8km)	1,625ft (495m)	3 hrs
16	Lord's Seat and Broom Fell	47	Whinlatter	NY 181 255	5¾ miles (9.4km)	1,755ft (535m)	3½ hrs
17	Pooley Bridge and Barton Park	50	Pooley Bridge	NY 469 245	6 miles (9.5km)	770ft (235m)	3 hrs
18	Tarn Hows	53	Hawkshead	SD 354 980	6 miles (9.5km)	985ft (300m)	3¼ hrs
19	Dent and Kinniside Stone Circle	56	Cleator Moor	NY 030 144	7 miles (11km)	1,575ft (480m)	4 hrs
20	Ennerdale	59	Ennerdale Bridge	NY 085 154	7 miles (11.5km)	655ft (200m)	3½ hrs
21	Wast Water	63	Wasdale	NY 151 054	8 miles (12.5km)	740ft (225m)	4 hrs
22	St Bees Head	67	St Bees	NX 961 117	8 miles (12km)	1,215ft (370m)	4¼ hrs
23	Crummock Water	71	Scalehill Bridge	NY 149 215	8½ miles (13.8km)	1,050ft (320m)	4¼ hrs
24	Dow Crag and Goat's Water	75	Torver	SD 285 944	7½ miles (11.9km)	2,395ft (730m)	4½ hrs
25	Place Fell	78	Patterdale	NY 396 159	7 miles (11.5km)	2,265ft (690m)	4½ hrs
26	Coledale Horseshoe	81	Stoneycroft	NY 232 217	9 miles (14.5km)	3,885ft (1,185m)	6 hrs
27	Wet Sleddale, Swindale and Mosedale	84	Wet Sleddale	NY 555 114	12½ miles (17.5km)	1,540ft (470m)	6 hrs
28	The Four Passes	88	Wasdale Head	NY 187 085	15 miles (24km)	4,430ft (1,350m)	9 hrs

Comments

An easy, if steep, ascent to an isolated fell of some geological uniqueness. Two variant circuits extend the options beyond a straight up-and-down walk.

Riparian exploration leads to an ancient hall and church set amid broad-leaved woodland; a perfect place for picnics.

A splendid and simple romp onto a superb ridge with outstanding views of Buttermere and the Vale of Lorton; fells, lakeshore and woodland provide the colours to what is a lovely scene.

An easy start around a beautiful tarn leads to rocky Side Pike; after skirting around its southern flank a simple ascent leads up to the summit of Lingmoor Fell.

A popular walk to one of Lakeland's finest waterfalls, but bolted on to a heady exploration of the craggy upland of Gowbarrow Fell above; concluding with a fine terrace path across steep fell slopes.

A simple enough walk, but one imbued with considerable historical interest that contrasts remarkably with the breezy openness of the moors of the Ralfland Forest of old.

A roundabout route to arguably the finest view of Mardale and Haweswater, linking two mountain passes and a fine outing across two high fells.

High Rigg is a delightful, undulating ridge largely ignored by walkers other than a discerning few. Numerous nooks and crannies offer shelter.

A pleasing circular walk through the Jaws of Borrowdale to a viewpoint made popular by a priest, and returning through broad-leaved woodlands in the company of the River Derwent.

A popular and hugely agreeable circuit of the heart of Wordsworth Country; where he lived, where he died, where he lies buried.

Launching itself from the tourist hotspot of Glenridding, the walk visits the site of the largest lead mine in the Lake District before skipping southwards into Grisedale by way of secluded Lanty's Tarn.

A dramatic and inspiring ascent to a lofty tarn, and craggy summits; wild and rugged scenery and views that will make the heart race with joy.

A popular walk through the woodland slopes of a comparatively lowly fell to a fine airy summit, now devoid of trees, and with extensive views of Bassenthwaite, Derwent Water and the fells beyond.

In spite of a fair amount of ascent, this visit to Greendale and adjacent fells is well worth the effort; a peaceful retreat with fine views and a splendid tarn beside which to relax.

One of the easiest Lakeland fells to attain, and one that gives a superb view into the moorland expanse that is 'Back o' Skidda' – wild and woolly, and visited by the connoisseurs of fell walking.

A splendid round of a remote dale to the highest summit of the North-Western Fells. A grassy romp follows before the walk concludes with a very steep descent to reach a secluded waterfall.

A lazy exploration along the shores of Ullswater and of the fells along its north-eastern flanks, rising onto open moorland inhabited by prehistoric man.

An unfamiliar approach to Tarn Hows, starting in the village where Wordsworth went to school, and making the most of splendid countryside.

A taste of the Coast-to-Coast walk, tackling its first (or last) summit, and then skittering down into a delectable hidden valley and visiting a reconstructed stone circle.

An easy walk on the wild side into the recesses of Ennerdale, beneath the gaze of Pillar.

An exhilarating crossing of the most famous screes in England, which fall into its deepest lake. The complexities of the scree traverse are contrasted by the ease on the opposite side of the lake.

A breezy romp above the cliffs north of St Bees following in the steps of the Coast-to-Coast Walk before taking its leave to pursue a gentle and pleasing return to the ancient settlement.

A long and delightful walk around Crummock Water that comes with the opportunity to visit Scale Force, the highest waterfall in the region. Excellent views of the Buttermere valley and the Vale of Lorton throughout.

An interesting and beautiful approach to an ancient cross-valley thoroughfare, followed by a splendid romp along a ridge before descending to a lovely tarn at the foot of the cliffs of Dow Crag.

Looming above the eastern side of Ullswater, Place Fell is often walked around rather than over; yet it offers superb views and is an exhilarating and energetic walk.

A fine high-level circuit of the Coledale valley that takes in several of Lakeland's finest and most distinctive fell summits.

A long and delightful circuit of the moors of Ralfland Forest, visiting remote dales and the location of a cult film.

A *tour de force* involving four Lakeland valleys and the passes that link them; yet in spite of the evident distance and height gain, the walking is generally straightforward.

Keymap

Introduction to More Lake District

The startling, perhaps most remarkable, thing about the Lake District is how so much can be crammed into what is really a fairly small space. The 885 sq miles (2,292 sq km) of the National Park may seem quite large, and you can spend many days driving round its various nooks and crannies without crossing your trail, but it remains remarkably compact. Stand on its highest summit, and you can see it all, from side to side: 33 miles (53km) from east to west, 40 miles (64km) north to south.

And it is this compactness that enthralls and surprises visitors, enabling them to zip from one delectable corner to another in a matter of minutes, or to stride purposefully across a fine mountain ridge, linking valleys, embracing new views almost with every stride. There is no 'sameness' about any of it; every bend in the road brings a new vista, a

Aira Force

mean of 497. The upland areas of Cumberland were equally thinly populated. A century or more earlier, the Lakeland valleys, peopled by '...humble sons of the hills', knew little of the influence of gentry, and bred an independence, stability and changelessness with authority vesting in the farming 'commonwealth' itself.

Where these Lakeland communities differed most noticeably from rural areas elsewhere in medieval and early-modern England was in the absence of landed gentry; there were few 'lords' influencing the way things developed. The consequence of this was that the landowners, many hovering between yeoman and gentleman and playing an important leadership role, directly controlled their own estates and prevented the transformation of the landscape that normally accompanied more widespread agricultural changes. This was a '...peaceful peasant world' founded on generations of custom and tradition, and home to a society that was deferential and democratic. The vast majority of Lakeland people lived by tilling the soil and tending flocks, the bulk of the land being held by a tenant right approximating to freehold possession. Where settlements occurred, they were scattered, small villages or hamlets. Wordsworth regarded this as a rural utopia; Thomas Gray as a '...little unsuspected paradise...[of] peace, rusticity and happy poverty'. The descriptions that flow through these

new twist in the trail, and panoply of stunning landscapes.

And it is the components of that landscape that serve to create a synergy of evolutionary liaisons that embraces so much to inspire and delight heart, mind and soul. Ironically, perhaps, for a place with a name based on lakes, there is but one 'official' lake – Bassenthwaite – all the others are tarns, meres, waters. But whatever you call them, these stretches of water are nationally important for their range of habitats, and collectively give the Lake District a unique quality of scenery and recreational resource that exceeds anything elsewhere in Britain.

For many years, the prevailing image of the Lake District was that of a peopled landscape. And yet, much of Cumbria was sparsely populated. As recently as 1891, Westmorland (one of the former counties) had a mean population of 81 persons per square mile, compared with a national and other accounts are hallmarked by observations of a people that worked hard and lived poorly, but for whom contentment, integrity and independence were no strangers.

Although more than 8 million people now visit the Lake District each year, it is home to fewer than 45,000 residents. And this sparseness of human population and the urban development that invariably goes with it, means that vast areas of open uplands – called 'fells' – carry an importance as a liberating and wilderness experience that is both distinctive and cherished.

Underfoot, the Lakeland rocks are among the oldest in Britain, providing a dramatic record of colliding continents, hugely deep oceans and tropical seas, and of ice sheets more than ½ mile (800m) thick. Lakeland, as a result,

collectively boasts the most impressive lakes in Britain, and the highest peaks in England, features that contribute to Man's understanding of our evolution and climatic past.

There is evidence of Man in the Lake District for more than 10,000 years, found in stone circles, burial mounds, axe factories and ancient field systems. What is less evident is the catalytic event that enabled Man to settle down instead of constantly moving on as hunter-gatherers – that event was farming, a development that enabled Man to produce food in one place, to put down roots in every sense. Today, the landscape reflects a long history of settlement, with more than 6,000 important archaeological sites and monuments dating from prehistory to the early part of the 20th century. Throw in over 200 scheduled

Tarn Hows and Black Fell

The summit of Gowbarrow Fell

ancient monuments, over 1,700 listed buildings and structures, and more than 20 Conservation Areas within its towns and villages, and Lakeland's depth of character becomes apparent.

The National Park area is host to the highest concentration of outdoor activity centres in the UK, the birthplace of mountaineering and rock climbing, and there has long been a tradition of unrestricted access to the fells, now ratified in law, along with a vast and complex network of rights of way. It is on this legacy that Pathfinder® guides are today based. They tap into the tranquillity of the lakes, the valleys and the soaring fells, exploring the aura of space and freedom, and providing a place of spiritual revival and a release from the brouhaha of everyday life.

So prized were the characteristics of the Lake District that it became necessary to protect them. Growing pressure from commerce and industry in the form of tourism, quarrying, water catchment and forestry, led to the formation of the Lake District Defence Society, founded in 1883, and a forerunner of the Friends of the Lake District. But for centuries, the Lake District as we know it was a debatable land, a frontier region haggled over by English and Scottish kings. For this reason, the region never made it into the Domesday survey initiated by William the Conqueror, and not until a strong fortress was established in Carlisle in 1092 was the frontier finally settled.

Following the Norman invasion, the fells and valleys of the Lakes came under the influence of monastic order, who came to own huge tracts of land and played an important part in the economic development of the region: clearing woodlands, developing sheep farms, excavating minerals and maintaining such roads as remained from the Roman occupation.

Today's visitors, bound for the fells, may not be aware of this remarkable history, but in the shape and lie of the land they are at one with it, striding through the pages of history, and eulogising as many others have done before them on the wonders and beauties that unfold.

Fifty years of exploring and writing about the Lake District by the author have still proven insufficient to see all its exquisite detail; there is always a peaceful retreat, a grassy bank by a crystal stream, a sheltered corner below a cliff high on Gable's shoulder, or a moment of quiet reflection by a fell tarn far from the world below. Such is the force of Lakeland's act, that it brings rave reviews from everyone, and choruses of the loudest acclaim. It is, as Wordsworth prophesised, '...a sort of national property, in which every man has a right and an interest who has an eye to perceive and a heart to enjoy.'

High Rigg Tarn

This book includes a list of waypoints alongside the description of the walk, so that you can enjoy the full benefits of gps should you wish to. For more information about route navigation, improving your map reading ability, walking with a GPS and for an introduction to basic map and compass techniques, read Pathfinder® Guide Navigation Skills for Walkers by outdoor writer Terry Marsh (ISBN 978-0-319-09175-3). This title is available in bookshops and online at shop.ordnancesurvey.co.uk

Cradled by the Esk, St Catherine's Church dates from the 12th century, when the Priory at St Bees owned a chapel here

Great Mell Fell

		GPS waypoints
Start	Near Matterdale End	
Distance	2 miles (3.5km)	NY 407 247
Height gain	855 feet (260m)	**A** NY 405 245
Approximate time	1½ hours (*variant 1*), 2 hours (*variant 2*)	**B** NY 401 250
Parking	Limited roadside parking at start	
Route terrain	Woodland track, open, grassy fellside	
Ordnance Survey maps	Landranger 90 (Penrith & Keswick), Explorer OL5 (The English Lakes – North-eastern area)	

The conquest of Great Mell Fell should faze no one; the fell is a simple, rounded dome, easy and delightful of access. A straightforward amble to the top and back is handsomely rewarding in itself. But turning the walk to the summit into either of the circular routes shown here involves an unavoidable, very steep descent. *Great Mell Fell and close neighbour Little Mell Fell share an interesting geology as carboniferous rocks form a comglomerate in which pebbles of Skiddaw slate, Borrowdale volcanics and Coniston limestone, among others, are set in a sandy matrix carried here by powerful floods and, resistant to erosion, they now form the smooth rounded fells visible today.*

The walk begins at a rough track leaving the road not far from Brownrigg Farm. Set off along the track, and continue past a National Trust Mell Fell sign at a gate, as this is not the way to

Great Mell Fell

go, in spite of it being rather inviting.

Stay on the stony track as far as the next gate on the right **A**. Pass through the gate and then bear left alongside a fence, climbing gently. For a while the path is flanked on the right by trees, but as these finally fall back you can leave the fence-side path by branching right onto a steeply ascending path.

A brief, leg-buckling climb soon eases a little, but the ascent continues, climbing past a number of wind-blown trees, and rising clearly through bracken. Eventually, you come on to the end of a very broad and rounded ridge. Here, swing left, still ascending but now more gently towards the left-hand edge of woodland.

SCALE 1:25000 or 2½ INCHES to 1 MILE 4CM to 1KM

| 0 | 200 | 400 | 600 | 800 METRES | 1 KILOMETRES |
| 0 | 200 | 400 | 600 YARDS | ½ MILES | |

before too long, leaving you to find the easiest gradient.

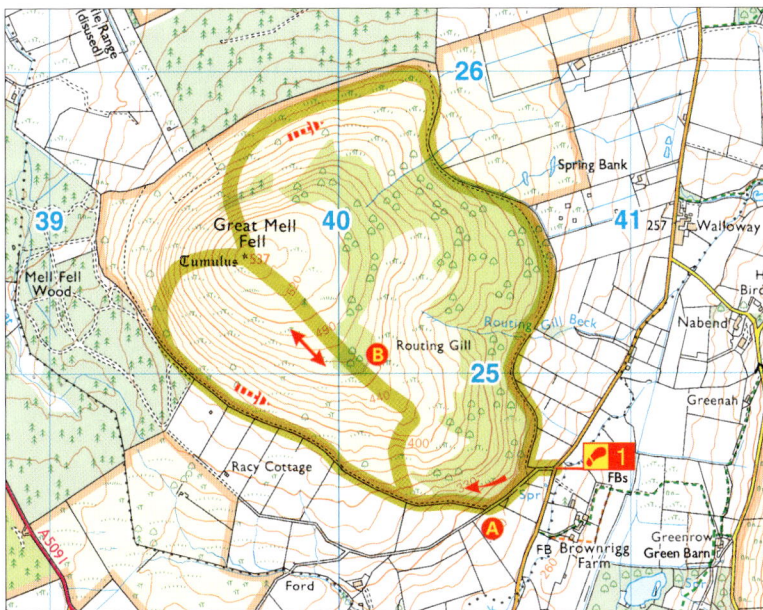

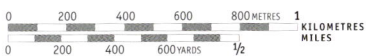

The path now above the bracken appears to lead directly into the trees, but then as you gain more height it bears left and passes through the end of the woodland **B**, mainly of Scots pine and larch. There is a fine view across Matterdale to the Dodds.

Just as you finally approach the summit, Blencathra eases into view. The top of Great Mell Fell is marked by a small cairn within a collapsed tumulus and on a fine day this is a truly wonderful place to be.

The surest return is now to retrace your steps because by any other route only very steep descents on grass (slippery when wet) await. Even so, those with the ability to deal with descents of this kind can add a little distance to the day.

Variant routes
From the top of Great Mell Fell, two indistinct grassy paths set off one roughly in a northerly direction, and the other roughly to the west. Both fade

1. *If you go west, the slope gradually steepens considerably, finally descending through gorse and bracken to reach a clear track running along the edge of Mell Fell Wood (partially cleared). Once the track is underfoot, simply turn left (south-east) and follow it back to the start. This option will add less than 200 yards to the overall walking distance.*

2. *If you decide to go north, then an equally steep descent awaits, also to the boundary of woodland, but this time there is no path of any note to reassure you. When you do reach the woodland boundary, simply turn right (north-east) and follow it almost to the eastern edge of the woodland where a good path is then encountered. Turn right (south) onto this, and take its sinuous course around the base of Great Mell Fell finally emerging at the National Trust sign encountered in the early stages of the walk. This option will increase the overall distance to 3 miles (4.8km), with 940 feet (335m) of height gain.* ●

Dalegarth and Eskdale

Start	Dalegarth
Distance	3 miles (5km)
Height gain	280 feet (85m)
Approximate time	1½ hours
Parking	Trough House Bridge
Route terrain	Woodland; riverside paths
Ordnance Survey maps	Landranger 89 (West Cumbria), Explorer OL6 (The English Lakes – South-western area)

GPS waypoints

- ✍ NY 172 003
- Ⓐ NY 172 001
- Ⓑ NY 188 004
- Ⓒ NY 189 007

An absolute gem of a walk; simple, delightful, easy and surrounded by extravagant beauty. This rewarding circuit should take less than two hours, but could just so easily waylay you for much more than that. Link it in with a ride on the miniature railway from Ravenglass, and you can enjoy a full day amid the most superb scenery.

✍ From the parking area at Trough House Bridge, where the Esk skitters through a scenic mélange of trees, rocks and bubbling streams, turn left to follow a surfaced lane to a bend opposite Dalegarth Hall.

Dalegarth Hall was built in 1599 (some say it dates from the 14th century), and boasts magnificent chimneys; it is the ancient manor house of Austhwaite, and home to the Stanley family.

Continue a short way farther to a track junction Ⓐ, and here turn left through a gate and follow a descending track across an enclosed pasture.

(Anyone wanting to visit Stanley Ghyll Force, a popular destination for adventurous Victorian travellers, should remain on the original track to view this dramatic fall in a deep and narrow gorge, and then return to the same point.)

After the next gate, cross a footbridge spanning a tributary of the Esk, which is close by. On exiting the woods, turn right along a broad track that swings

left across rough ground, with St Catherine's Church putting in an appearance through the trees on your left.

The track wanders on through a delightful thin belt of woodland much favoured by great spotted woodpeckers. Keep on to reach a small tarn, surrounded by larch, and with a convenient bench on which to rest and reflect for a while. A few strides beyond the bench, leave the stony track by bearing left along a grassy path with a waymarker post beside it.

Another footbridge spans a busy beck, after which the track runs on to Low Birker Farm, with lovely views to the left of Scafell, Slight Side and the nearer shapely profiles of Great and Little Barrow. On nearing Low Birker Ⓑ, descend left on a stony track that passes to the left of the buildings, and then walk along the access track to arrive at the single span of Doctor Bridge Ⓒ.

Cross the bridge and turn left on the

SCALE 1:25000 or 2½ INCHES to 1 MILE 4CM to 1KM

| 0 | 200 | 400 | 600 | 800 METRES | 1 |
| 0 | 200 | 400 | 600 YARDS | ½ | |

KILOMETRES
MILES

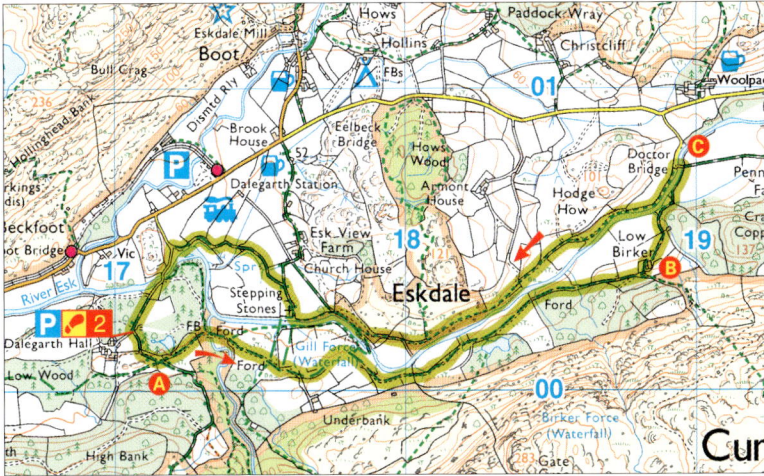

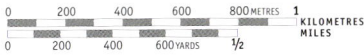

other side, through a gate and along a path for St Catherine's Church. You soon reach a riverside bench, which would be a perfect place for a picnic.

The return path is every bit as delightful and straightforward as the outward leg, with the added attraction that it passes a fascinating display of dry-stone walls. After a short stretch between such walls, the path breaks out into a rough grassy pasture dotted with gorse and bracken, and later becomes a fine terraced path across a steep bank

Eskdale landscape

above the river.

Having ignored two trails signposted to the right, the path eventually comes back down to run beside the river again. At a fork, bear left through the gate to reach St Catherine's Church. Cradled by the Esk, St Catherine's Church dates from the 12th century, when the Priory at St Bees owned a chapel here. It is an enchanting setting, particularly in early spring when the graveyard is covered in daffodils.

Take the walled track to the right of the church, but after about 100 yards, turn left onto an enclosed path, which eventually emerges to meet a surfaced lane. Turn left to return to Trough House Bridge, and complete the walk. ●

Rannerdale Knotts

Start	Buttermere
Distance	3 miles (4.5km)
Height gain	1,015 feet (310m)
Approximate time	2 hours
Parking	National Trust car park (Pay and Display)
Route terrain	Steep, grassy fell slopes, up and down, stone-pitched descent
Ordnance Survey maps	Landranger 89 (West Cumbria), Explorer OL4 (The English Lakes – North-western area)

GPS waypoints

🖊 NY 172 172
Ⓐ NY 178 177
Ⓑ NY 167 177

Rannerdale Knotts offers a short but hugely delightful ridge walk from the village of Buttermere. This diminutive summit offers stunning views of Buttermere lake, Crummock Water and Loweswater. The return leg touches on the shoreline of Crummock Water and passes through Nether How woodland. There is a view into the 'Secret Valley', where battles raged in centuries gone by.

🖊 Leave the National Trust car park and cross the road to take to a narrow grassy path on the other side heading gently and then steeply uphill. As the gradient steepens considerably, take the left-hand path, which leads up to a shallow linking col Ⓐ between the Rannerdale ridge and Whiteless Pike.

Rannerdale Knotts across Crummock Water

This is a great place to take a breather and admire the view.

Turn left (westwards) onto the ridge, and follow its gently rising course to the neat and shapely topknot of Rannerdale, another fine viewpoint.

From the summit, follow the narrow, winding track on your left, downhill towards the lake. The initial path soon reaches a steep, stone-pitched stretch that *can be very slippery when wet*. Once this is behind you, follow the descending track until it branches left, and then makes a more gentle descent in a south-easterly direction to the road Ⓑ.

Cross the road, and pass through a gate to the lakeshore, walking beside the lake until you

Cinderdale Common and Grasmoor

see a gate on the left giving into Nether How woods. Follow the path beyond the gate into the woodland, briefly touching on the lakeshore again before returning to woodland cover. Now take the path to your left through the wood to a footbridge.

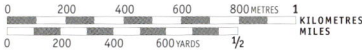

Cross the bridge, and follow the ongoing path to complete the walk. ●

Side Pike and Lingmoor Fell

		GPS waypoints
Start	Blea Tarn	
Distance	2¾ miles (4.4km)	🖊 NY 296 043
Height gain	1,005 feet (305m)	Ⓐ NY 289 051
		Ⓑ NY 294 053
Approximate time	2 hours	Ⓒ NY 303 046
Parking	National Trust car park, Blea Tarn (Pay and Display)	
Route terrain	Rough fell country	
Ordnance Survey maps	Landranger 90 (Penrith & Keswick), Explorer OL6 (The English Lakes – South-western area)	

For many visitors, Blea Tarn set against the backdrop of Pike o'Blisco on the one hand and Lingmoor Fell on the other, is a perfect vision of Lakeland. That it rests in a little hanging valley between the two Langdale valleys, and is approachable only along narrow, twisting and bumpy roads makes it all the more appealing. The tarn is the starting point for this short but endearing encounter with fell walking.

🖊 On leaving the car park, cross the road and walk down the gravel path opposite that leads around the southern edge of the tarn. Go through a gate and, on crossing a footbridge spanning the outflow from the tarn, turn immediately

Blea Tarn and Side Pike

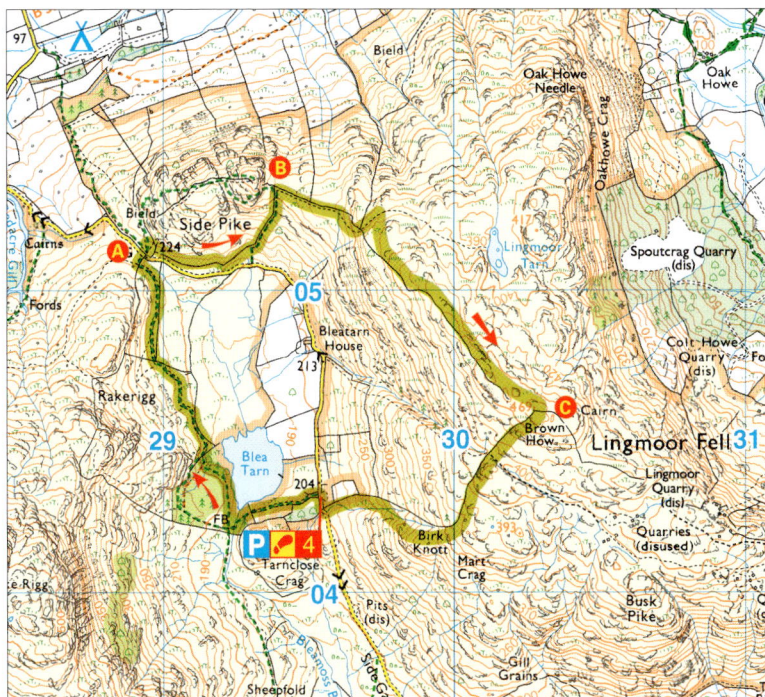

SCALE 1:25000 or 2½ INCHES to 1 MILE 4CM to 1KM

0	200	400	600	800 METRES	1
					KILOMETRES
					MILES
0	200	400	600 YARDS	½	

right along a continuing path that runs up the west side of the tarn, and leaves the National Trust grounds at another gate farther on.

Now simply follow a clear and broad track northwards until you arrive at the road, near a cattle grid **A**.

For the geologically minded, Side Pike is something of a rarity in the ancient geological record in that it exhibits the three main categories of pyroclastic rock: fallout, surge and flow deposits. Moreover, the rocks found here helped scientists to determine the non-marine nature of the principal rocks, those of the Borrowdale Volcanic Series.

Cross the road and go through a gate to a junction of four radiating paths. Take the one going right, which simply loops around the craggy upthrust of Side Pike before climbing beside a fence to meet a wall corner **B**.

Turn right and walk with a wall on your left, as you start the ascent of Lingmoor Fell. The path leads up to a wall corner, where you cross a step stile in an adjacent fence, and then take an ascending path diagonally on the right, which soon doubles back to run beside a wall.

By sticking with the wall/fence, you are guided unerringly up to the summit of Lingmoor Fell **C**, marked by a large cairn.

Here, cross a simple step stile on the right to begin the return to the Blea Tarn car park. Stay alongside a fence and wall throughout the descent, although at one point the path moves away from the wall for a while.

When you reach an area of scattered juniper bushes close by a stream, bear right again to cross back towards the wall besides which a path leads down to the road, reaching it just to the south of the car park. Cross the cattle grid to return to the start. ●

Aira Force and Gowbarrow Park

		GPS waypoints
Start	Patterdale, south of Dockray	NY 401 201
Distance	4 miles (6.5km)	**A** NY 399 215
Height gain	1,250 feet (380m)	**B** NY 414 217
Approximate time	2½ hours	**C** NY 412 206
Parking	Aira Force car park at start (Pay and Display)	
Route terrain	Managed parkland; open fell tops; steep slopes	
Ordnance Survey maps	Landranger 90 (Penrith & Keswick), Explorer OL5 (The English Lakes – North-eastern area)	

Drawing its waters from the grassy folds of Deepdale, Aira Force is one of Lakeland's most admired waterfalls, the showpiece of a fine display of cataracts, tumbling water and deep pools. In this walk, a visit to the Force is combined with a wide, sweeping circuit of Gowbarrow Park, formerly a medieval deer park, and retaining stretches of bleak, rock-punctuated moorland dotted with gnarled oak trees.

Leave the Aira Force car park at its northern end, and pass through an opening near an information panel, to follow a path above Aira Beck. When the path forks, just after having crossed a minor stream, bear left to pass some fine specimens of yew, and, a short way farther on, a money tree.

The ongoing path climbs steadily, with the beck bustling away below. As you approach the Force, invariably heard before it is seen, you pass a flight of steps down to the base of the main waterfall. Go down to appreciate the falls, but then return to the top of the steps to resume the original route. The path now leads up and round to a point high above Aira Force, with steps leading down to a bridge spanning the topmost part of the falls.

Cross the Force bridge, and take the first path rising briefly on your left, upstream, along the true left bank of the beck, but almost immediately quit this by climbing onto a low shoulder on the right, to a path that leads up to a step stile. Over the stile, take the path swinging to the left.

At another stile you enter light woodland of birch, hazel and oak, and press on across the top of a flight of steps that leads down to a footbridge. Staying on the continuing path through the woodland you arrive at a higher waterfall, High Force; less dramatic than Aira Force below, but nevertheless (literally) a force to be reckoned with, its banks a delightful place for a breather.

Above High Force, the path, now signed for Dockray and Ulcat Row, continues through a wall gap and a little more woodland. Follow this through

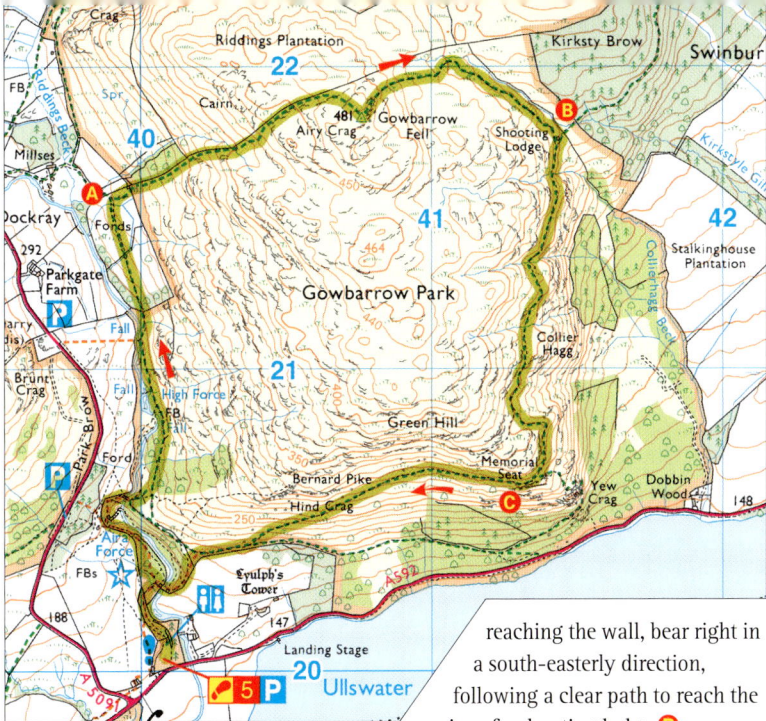

Map labels: Crag, Riddings Plantation, Kirksty Brow, Swinbur, FB, Spr, 22, Cairn, 481, Gowbarrow Fell, Airy Crag, Shooting Lodge, **B**, Millses, 40, **A**, Dockray, Fonds, 292, Parkgate Farm, 41, 42, Stalkinghouse Plantation, Gowbarrow Park, arry, dis), Fall, Brunt Crag, Fall, High Force, 21, FB, Ford, Collier Hagg, Green Hill, Memorial Seat, Bernard Pike, Hind Crag, Yew Crag, Dobbin Wood, 148, **C**, Aira Force, FBs, Lyulph's Tower, 88, 147, Landing Stage, 20, **5 P**, Ullswater

SCALE 1:25 000 or 2½ INCHES to 1 MILE 4CM to 1KM

```
0   200   400   600   800 METRES   1
                                    KILOMETRES
                                    MILES
0   200   400   600 YARDS   ½
```

thinning trees, passing a wall before reaching open bracken heath. Cross this towards a wall on the far side, but before reaching it, turn right **A** to use a gate in the wall ahead, to begin a steady pull up onto Gowbarrow Fell.

The ascending path stays close by a wall, and the opportunity should be taken to pause numerous times to take in the view along the length of Ullswater, and across the Dockray dip to the burgeoning fells of Matterdale Common, rising to Great Dodd. Sheffield Pike peers above the top of Watermillock Common.

Eventually, the path moves away from the wall and bears right to climb to the trig pillar of Gowbarrow Fell, now conspicuous on the skyline.

Cross the top of the fell, *taking care on what proves to be a slippery descent on the other side, especially after rain.* The path continues descending towards a wall beyond which the darkness of Swinburn's Park looms. But before

reaching the wall, bear right in a south-easterly direction, following a clear path to reach the ruins of a shooting lodge **B**.

At the lodge you intercept a right of way. Go right, following it roughly in a southerly direction as it climbs slightly to cross three streams all feeding into Collierhagg Beck and Ullswater. This is a superb traverse, *but crosses steep slopes that may deter anyone suffering from vertigo,* but which are not generally a problem. When the path divides (indistinctly), take the prominent left branch, dropping a little before swinging right round a corner with the top of Yew Crag, a cairned viewpoint, in sight, below and to your left. Stay above the crag, and pass a memorial seat **C**, then simply follow the path, heading steadily downwards, and finally bear left back into the woodland in the Aira Force grounds just above a noticeable building close by the road below, Lyulph's Tower.

Back within the Aira Force grounds, bear left and take a path that descends to a footbridge. On the other side, climb steps and then bear left, soon to rejoin your outward route, close by the clearing containing yew trees. Simply retrace your steps to the start. ●

Shap Abbey

Start	Shap
Distance	4½ miles (7.5km)
Height gain	425 feet (130m)
Approximate time	2 hours
Parking	Shap
Route terrain	Farmland; moorland; some road walking
Ordnance Survey maps	Landranger 90 (Penrith & Keswick), Explorer OL5 (The English Lakes – North-eastern area)

GPS waypoints

- NY 563 151
- **A** NY 545 143
- **B** NY 539 152
- **C** NY 539 155

Shap Abbey is a key feature of this walk, a gaunt and evocative ruin on the banks of the River Lowther. But there is more interest besides, not least a huge monolith encountered early in the walk, a small but attractive village and acres of wild moorland where the air is laced with skylark trill and curlew-speak.

Set off from the car park and turn right, walking along Main street (the A6), as far as a turning on the left at the fire station.

Shap is a place of some antiquity, having been granted a market charter in 1687; the odd-shaped market hall with curious windows and round arches stands on the main road, near the start of the walk; much of the stone for its building came from nearby Shap abbey following the Dissolution of the

Shap Abbey

Monasteries. With motorway traffic thundering along not that far distant, it is difficult to believe now that this was the main thoroughfare between north and south, and that in winter it was often impassable.

The area around Shap has been inhabited since prehistoric times as standing stones and remains of stone circles testify. To the south of the village, **Shap Wells Hotel** was built in the 1830s to replace a small and somewhat indifferent inn that served the needs of visitors coming to 'take the waters' at Shap spa. Although never on a par with Bath or Buxton, Shap Wells had its share of fame and attracted numerous members of the aristocracy. During the Second World War, the hotel was used as a prisoner of war camp for senior Luftwaffe and naval officers.

Turn left at the fire station and then first left, crossing to a footpath signpost directing you up an enclosed area at the rear of houses. This gives into a sloping, limestone-walled field at the top of which High Street, Kidsty Pike and the high fells on either side come into view. Head downfield now to a gap stile in a corner that feeds you into another, this time narrow, walled path, issuing then into a field in the middle of which stands a huge stone.

The Goggleby Stone is part of what little remains of an avenue of standing stones from Kemp Howe Stone Circle to the south (largely destroyed by the West Coast Mainline Railway), to a barrow farther north. Most of this avenue was destroyed at the time of the enclosure of common land (1760–1820), but a few remain. The Goggleby Stone is one such; another is the Thunder Stone (NY 551 157).

Keep forward alongside a wall, and on the far side of the field you intercept an old, walled track. Cross this and continue on a grassy path across two more fields. The path leads to a stile

giving onto the narrow lane down to Keld, but it is possible to stay within the field boundary for a little while longer, although the stile exiting the field at the edge of Keld is rather more awkward to negotiate; better to leave the field at the earlier opportunity, and walk down the lane. As you enter Keld, you encounter its medieval chapel, a squat, rectangular structure shoe-horned into a wedge of ground, and thought to date from the 15th century, when it was probably a chantry attached to Shap Abbey. This lovely, stone-built structure is now in the ownership of the National Trust, its interior of the most simple and rustic kind.

Press on through the village and out along a continuing lane leading onto the moorland beyond. Soon, you cross the River Lowther. Stay on the surfaced lane as you approach another bridge, with Shap Abbey tucked into the folds of the landscape off to your right. Even farther distant, you can pick out the undulating summits of the high

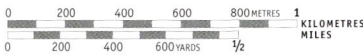

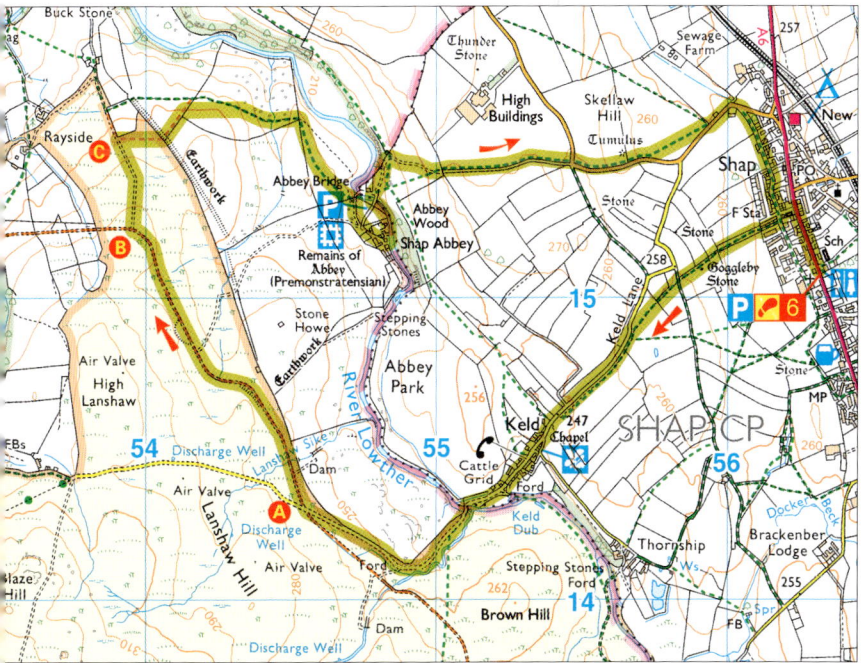

SCALE 1:25000 or 2½ INCHES to 1 MILE 4CM to 1KM

Keld chapel

Pennines, culminating in Cross Fell.

Eventually, you intercept another track **A**, a concrete service road. Here turn right for Rayside. The road ultimately leads over the moors to Mardale, and sweeps on across tussocky, reedy moorland. The sense of openness and freedom is superb.

At the next junction **B**, turn right down a rough-surfaced track towards Rayside. Follow the lane as far as a wall on the right **C**. Here, leave the lane for a boggy path across rough pasture leading to a gate at a wall corner. Go forward alongside a wall, and after about 100 yards, turn a wall corner, climbing a little, but then letting the wall guide you down through a dip and on to a ladder stile in a field corner.

Having crossed the ladder stile you find the River Lowther once more, and can cross a sloping pasture towards Shap Abbey. The path guides you to a steep bank overlooking a loop in the river. A path does descend the bank, but it is safer to stay above it and walk round to a stile, which avoids having to dodge overhanging branches.

Cross the stile, and go forward to visit the abbey. Shap Abbey, originally built at the very end of the 12th century, was among the last to be closed by Henry VIII. It belonged to an order founded by the German saint, Norbert, and owes its foundation to a baron named Thomas son of Gospatric. Very little is known about the history of the abbey. The order was of Premonstratensian monks and intended for those who wished to combine the life of prayer and discipline with parish work as priests serving local communities. Such men were known as White Canons from the colour of the habits they wore.

The end for Shap came on 14 January 1540, when the last abbot surrendered the abbey's possessions to the representatives of the Crown.

On leaving, cross the river by either of two bridges, and then follow a surfaced access lane that climbs across sloping pasture to a cattle grid. You can now simply follow the walled lanes back to Shap, but these are seasonally busy roads, and there is a safer alternative available. Beside the cattle grid, go through a gated gap stile in a wall corner and follow a wall-side path across a field (although there is no path underfoot), to emerge at a bend where the abbey road meets the Shap–Bampton road. Cross the road and go through a gate opposite, to repeat the wallside walk, crossing an intermediate wall at a corner before heading down to rejoin the road at a gate in the bottom right-hand corner. Near that intermediate wall, a raised mound of grass is a recorded tumulus, possibly Bronze Age.

Turn left along the road towards Shap, but as it bends to the right, leave it for a lovely walled path on the right. This leads you behind houses and on to reach an estate road opposite West Close, where you began the walk. Now turn left to the main road, and then right to return to the car park. ●

Nannycatch Beck

Adam Seat and Harter Fell

		GPS waypoints
Start	Mardale Head	📌 NY 469 107
Distance	4½ miles (7.2km)	Ⓐ NY 474 092
Height gain	1,755 feet (535m)	Ⓑ NY 459 093
Approximate time	3 hours	Ⓒ NY 452 096
Parking	Mardale Head	
Route terrain	Rough, stony fell tracks and summits; steep descent	
Ordnance Survey maps	Landranger 90 (Penrith & Keswick), Explorer OL5 (The English Lakes – North-eastern area)	

Mardale is a beautiful retreat, flanked by fine fells, and, if you want to be maudlin, with a sad story to tell. The people who settled here and remained until the 1930s, in spite of their undoubted hardships, must have known they were living somewhere special. And it is heartening to think that from time to time those long-dead shepherds might have wandered up onto the fells and gazed down on their valley home with just a smattering of contentment. There is no finer place for taking in the whole dale than the top of Harter Fell. This fine, short but energetic circuit around the head of Mardale uses two ancient packhorse trail crossing points – Gatescarth and Nan Bield passes – running north to south across the high fells.

📌 Set off through the gate at Mardale Head and take the path rising on the left, a stony trod that climbs steadily, zigzagging when to do so eases the gradient, all the way to the fence and gate at the top of Gatescarth Pass

Mardale Head

Ⓐ. This is an ancient thoroughfare, and would have seen regular use by packhorse trains in the 18th and 19th centuries.

Just before reaching the top of the pass, a broad track sweeps upwards on the right. This relatively new trail leads directly to Harter Fell, passing first over the craggy upthrust of Little Harter Fell. But, instead of taking this popular way, climb in a south-westerly direction alongside the fence following a grassy path to the summit of Adam Seat. Here the view opens up southwards down the great valley of Longsleddale and across the Shap Fells to Tarn Crag and Gray Crag, and towards hidden Crookdale.

The summit of Adam Seat is marked

```
0      200    400    600    800 METRES   1
                                         KILOMETRES
                                         MILES
0      200    400    600 YARDS   ½
```

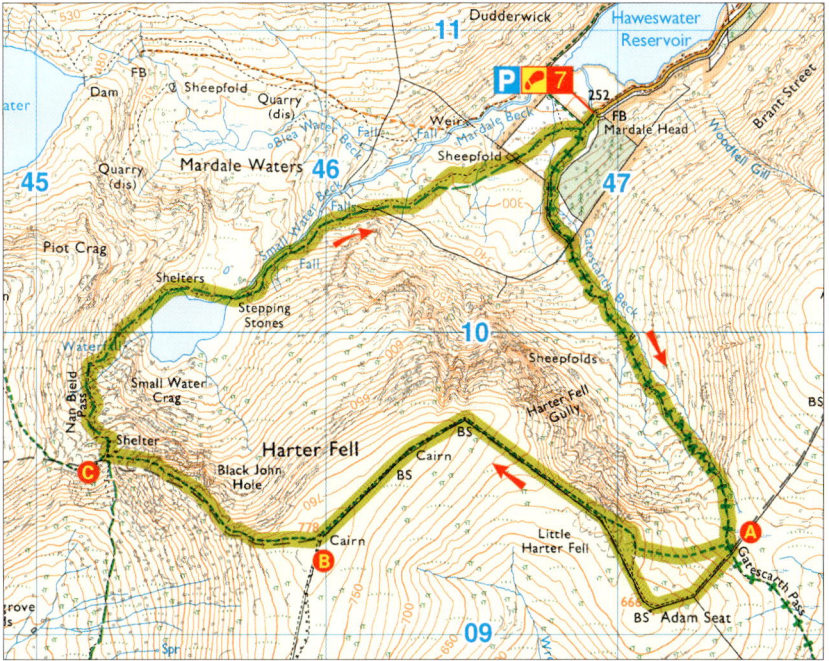

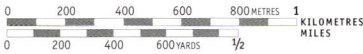

by a fine steeple-like marker bearing the letters 'L', on one side and 'H' on the side facing Kendal. The first is clearly for Lowther, the second letter's significance however is not clear, perhaps the Howards of Greystoke.

Press on beside the fence and eventually join a broad stony track that leads up to the summit of Harter Fell **B**.

Harter Fell

On the way, and just after the fenceline changes direction, a cairn marks the finest view of Mardale.

From the top of Harter Fell, you set off in a westerly direction, descending steeply on a clear path through rocky terrain until you reach the Nan Bield Pass **C**, where there is a small shelter. Like Gatescarth, this, too, is an ancient packhorse trail crossing point.

At the pass, you now turn northwards and descend around Small Water, following a clear and mainly stony path back down to Mardale Head. ●

High Rigg and St John's in the Vale

		GPS waypoints
Start	Legburthwaite	
Distance	5 miles (8km)	🖊 NY 318 195
Height gain	1,215 feet (370m)	Ⓐ NY 311 209
Approximate time	3 hours	Ⓑ NY 306 225
Parking	Legburthwaite (Pay and Display)	Ⓒ NY 314 213
Route terrain	Undulating fell ridge; rock outcrops and grass; farmland; riverside path	
Ordnance Survey maps	Landranger 90 (Penrith & Keswick), Explorer OL5 (The English Lakes – North-eastern area)	

High Rigg is a wedge of upland sandwiched between the bulk of High Seat and Castlerigg Fell to the west, and the Dodds beyond St John's Beck to the east. As a walking ground it is quite splendid, and largely ignored. The real beauty is that its many undulations and rocky outcrops are a canvas on which numerous ways can be drawn, the simplest being to follow the high ground. This walk describes such a high-level route, but you can virtually explore indiscriminately and find many sheltered nooks in which to wile away the hours contemplating the northern horizon of Skiddaw and Blencathra, or the crags of Clough Head to the east. Turn round and you can follow a route all the way up onto Helvellyn.

🖊 The car park at Legburthwaite is a perfect starting point, and from it you leave by a narrow gate giving onto an old, now gated, road. Turn left and walk out to the A591; there turn right, crossing a road bridge over St John's Beck, and shortly leaving the road at a gate and stile giving into the southern edge of the High Rigg domain.

A clear path now starts the ascent onto High Rigg. Shortly, when the path divides, branch left and simply follow its upward course, climbing steeply, among Scots pine. The steepness is relatively short-lived and the top of the

first main rise is a good place to take in the surroundings, among which the craggy bulk of Castle Rock of Triermain is most prominent, protruding from the lower slopes of Watson's Dodd.

Castle Rock, long popular with rock gymnasts, was described by Walter Scott as the setting for his poem *The Bridal of Triermain*, in which he tells how the knight, Sir Roland, besieges the enchanted castle in search of the daughter of King Arthur and the Fairy Queen. He wrote: '... midmost of the vale, a mound Arose which airy turrets crown'd, Buttress, and rampire's circling

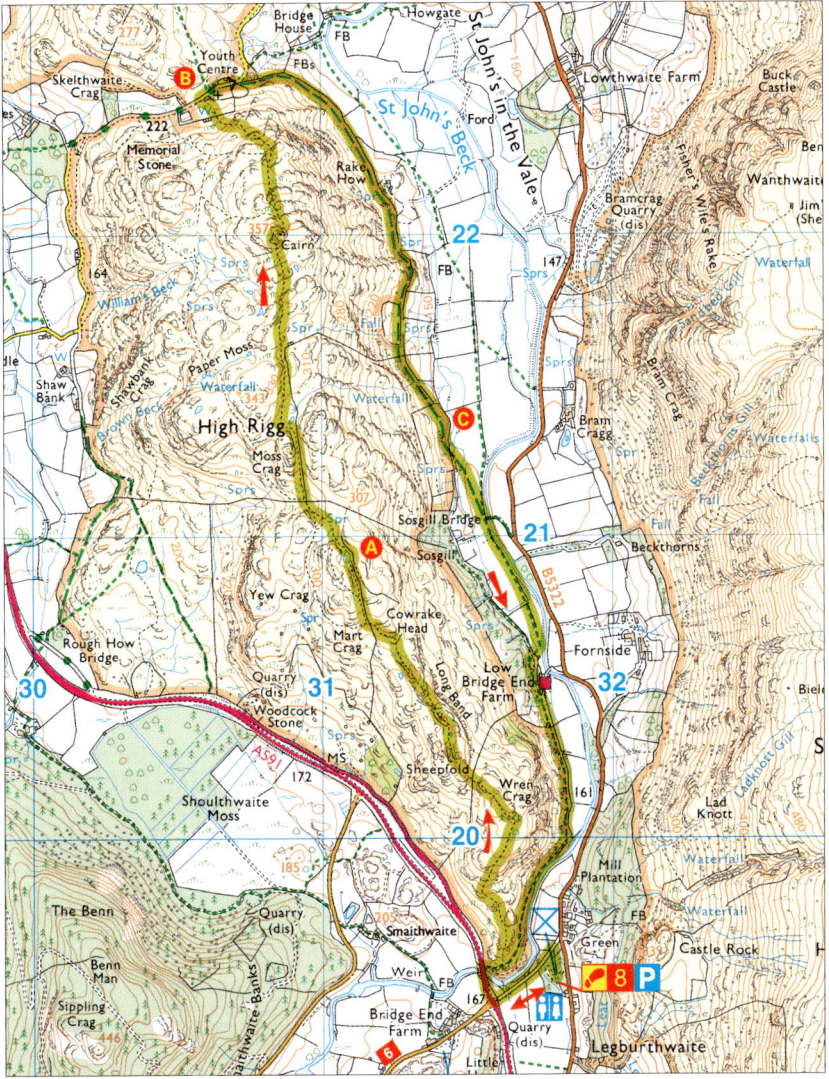

SCALE 1:25 000 or 2½ INCHES to 1 MILE 4CM to 1KM

0	200	400	600	800 METRES	1	
						KILOMETRES
						MILES
0	200	400	600 YARDS	½		

bound, And mighty keep and tower;
Seem'd some primeval giant's hand, The
castle's massive walls had plann'd, A
ponderous bulwark ...'

The main path is never in doubt, and
slips down to pass through a wall gap,
beyond which a little scrambly shoulder
takes you to a fine viewpoint north
along the bumpy ridge – exactly what
the word 'rigg' means. And as you pass

through the long and delightful
succession of dips so you can watch the
mountains rise again and again; or turn
about to gaze upon Helvellyn, its lower
flanks now cleared of overbearing
roadside trees. Thirlmere fills the dale,
flanked to the west by cloaks of pine
above which majestic Raven Crag puts
on a defiant show. It is all very inspiring
and, now that the ridge has been
gained, walking of the finest kind.

*When the path intercepts a fence at a
step stile, you have the choice of*

Looking north along High Rigg

sticking to the main path, which will lead you round and onward to meet a ladder stile at a wall junction; or cross the stile and immediately turn right to walk beside a fence, past a small tarn **Ⓐ**. It is worth walking up onto the knoll above the tarn, for then the tarn features in a lovely picture of Clough Head; to do this, leave the fence-side path just as it levels, and branch left onto marginally higher ground, from which there are numerous ways of returning to the tarn. Un-named, but not unreasonably High Rigg Tarn, this small lake ringed by bogbean and rushes, is the only one of High Rigg's many small tarns that does not dry up seasonally.

Beyond the tarn, you gradually descend to a wall junction, where the regular path re-appears. Cross a ladder stile here, and walk up beside a wall. The path moves away to pass around the end of a small, boggy area. Again there is the choice of doubling back towards the wall, or of heading onto higher ground.

As the wall changes direction, simply keep forward to reach the top of High Rigg, a perfect crown, topped by a cairn of modest girth. From the summit a path tumbles northwards to the church of St John's in the Vale **Ⓑ**, lying, almost unseen from above, along the narrow road that here crosses the fell, and that was once a main thoroughfare linking the dales on either side. Beyond this hiatus, the ridge continues northwards to blue-eyed Tewet Tarn. Reaching the church-side road, turn right, and descend a short distance until, just after the end of the graveyard, you can leave the road at a gate for a broad track, a bridleway, that now provides a simple, mildly undulating, and very therapeutic scamper southwards, high above St John's Beck.

The onward route is straightforward, and leads to Low Bridge End Farm. As you head towards the farm you first encounter a swathe of woodland. Before reaching it, keep an eye open for a single arch bridge that seems to be floating in the middle of a pasture on your left. A gate **Ⓒ** gives access to the pasture and an indistinct path leads towards the bridge (Sosgill Bridge). Just on reaching the bridge, and without crossing it, turn right onto the top of a flood embankment that leads on beside St John's Beck to the edge of Low Bridge End Farm.

Pass a large open barn, and then bear right on a path that takes you round the edge of the farm, which, for those in need of refreshment, will be found to have a small **tea garden**. Beyond the farm the path drops to become a broad path alongside a wall, there is every likelihood that this is an old Church Path. Castle Rock looms ahead, as the path climbs above the beck before running out to meet the A591 again, rejoining the outward route. Turn left and shortly left again along the old road to return to the car park. ●

Castle Crag and the Jaws of Borrowdale

		GPS waypoints
Start	Seatoller	
Distance	5 miles (8km)	
Height gain	820 feet (250m)	
Approximate time	3 hours	
Parking	Seatoller	
Route terrain	Stony tracks, riverside paths, many tree roots and short rocky stretches	
Ordnance Survey maps	Landranger 90 (Penrith & Keswick), Explorer OL4 (The English Lakes – North-western area)	

GPS waypoints

- NY 246 138
- **A** NY 242 141
- **B** NY 248 159
- **C** NY 250 165
- **D** NY 251 151

It was the raw vision of Castle Crag, stark against the brooding mountains beyond, that prompted early visitors to the Lakes to describe what is actually a geological constriction as the 'Jaws of Borrowdale'; emotive language symptomatic of a time when the mountains were fearful places inhabited by dragons. There are no dragons there now, and Castle Crag turns out to be an excellent vantage point.

Leave the car park and turn right at the road to walk up through the village of Seatoller. Most of the houses here are 17th-century and were built for workers employed at the nearby quarry on Honister Pass and in plumbago mines (a mineral used in dyeing, pencils and medicine). Nearby Seatoller House is the annual venue for the Lake Hunts, a sporting tradition inspired by the man hunt in Robert Louis Stevenson's *Kidnapped,* and originally started as a game of hare and hounds in 1898 by three Cambridge undergraduates – G. M. Trevelyan, Geoffrey Winthrop Young and Sidney McDougall.

At the edge of the village, turn right at a gate giving onto a clear track that climbs easily onto the fellside above, and then swings left to a gate. Beyond the gate continue climbing along a stony track, initially beside a wall, until it encounters a steeper path coming up from Seatoller. Go ahead onto the middle one of three possible paths, and walk across close-cropped turf to a wall corner and gate **A**.

Through the gate, turn right alongside a wall onto a path that leads on steadily, crossing streams by footbridges to reach the foot of Tongue Gill, a pronounced and deeply cleft ravine on the left, once a scene of much quarrying activity. Having gained height, the path now affords an airy view of Borrowdale and its ring of fells. The valley base is characterised by fecund green pastures that occupy an area which was once covered by shallow glacial lakes.

After Tongue Gill, the path, obvious and well-trodden throughout, heads for

Castle Crag directly ahead and framed between distant views of Skiddaw and Blencathra.

As you draw level with Castle Crag **B**, the track begins to descend, but you can pick out a path rising on the right just before an enormous spill of scree. If you want to visit the top of Castle Crag, this is the way to go. So, leave the main track and cross to the path onto the crag, rising steeply, very steeply in places, onto Castle Crag, now in the ownership of the National Trust.

People have been hauling themselves to the top of Castle Crag for centuries; this was one of Thomas West's 'Stations' to which visitors were guided to gain the best views of the surrounding countryside. In his *Guide to the Lakes,* first published in 1778, West describes the outlook from the crag '... a most astonishing view of the lake and vale of Keswick, spread out to the north in the most picturesque manner. From the pass of Borrowdale, every bend of the river, till it joins the lake, is distinctly seen; the lake itself, spotted with islands; the most extraordinary line of shore, varied with all the surprising accompaniments [sic] of rocks and woods ... To the south ... the river is seen winding from the lake upward, through the rugged pass, to where it divides and embraces a triangular vale, completely cut into inclosures of meadow, enamelled with softest verdure, and fields waving with fruitful crops ... This truly secreted spot is completely surrounded by the most horrid, romantic mountain in this region of wonders.'

Descend carefully from Castle Crag, rejoin the main track and turn right, heading downhill into the confines of Low Hows Wood. After a gate into the woodland, a footbridge crosses a stream that tumbles to the River Derwent below. On reaching the river, turn right onto a path for Rosthwaite **C**, now heading back towards Seatoller. The path meanders almost as lazily as the river, through lovely woodland, sometimes close by the river, at others farther away, but never in doubt. Shortly after turning left at a signpost for Rosthwaite, you pass an old quarry, *but it is not safe to explore.*

Eventually, the path breaks free of the woodland and follows an easy route to a neat, single-arched bridge, New Bridge **D**. Do not cross the bridge, but opt instead for a nearby footbridge, followed by another, after which you

Castle Crag, Borrowdale, from beside the River Derwent

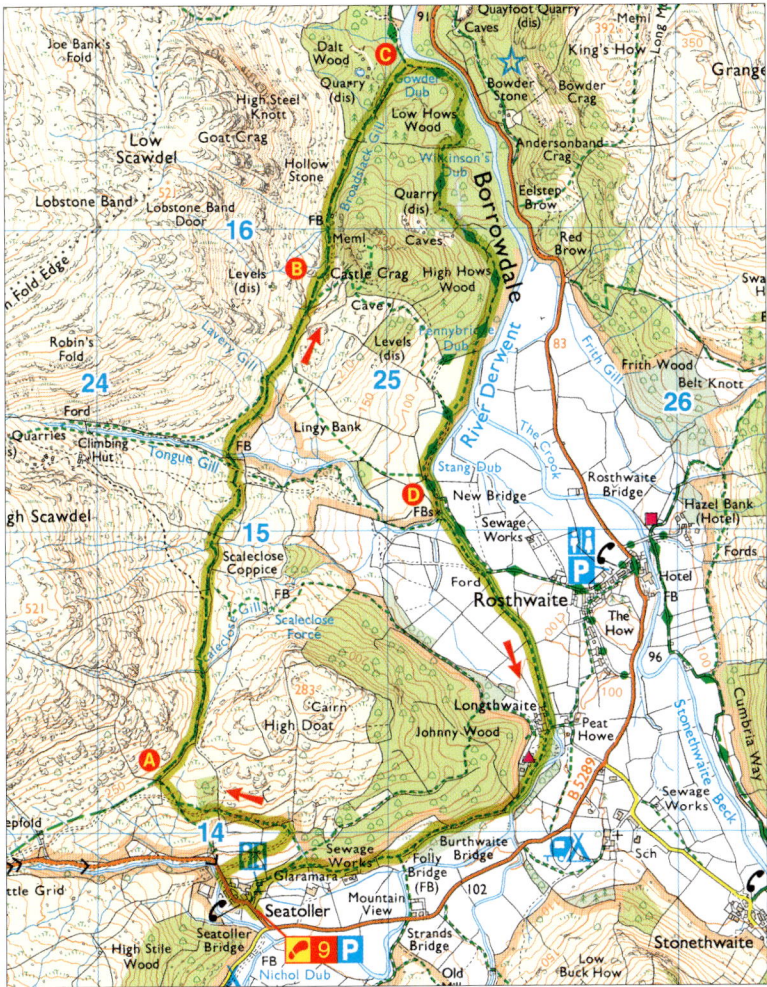

take to a narrow path parallel with the river and alongside a fence. At a gate you reach stepping stones spanning the river. Ignore them, and continue beside a wall initially crossing many tree roots that can be *slippery when wet*. Stay alongside the river, and press on to a kissing-gate from which you pass a cottage onto a track to a surfaced lane. Here, turn right towards Borrowdale Youth Hostel.

Pass in front of the hostel, and then keep forward, still beside the river, following a broad track. Stay ahead through an awkward rocky section, just where the river changes direction. A short section of glaciated rock has chains attached for security, welcome if the rocks are wet. Just after this, descend briefly to the left and then go immediately right, over a rocky shoulder to gain a fence-side path leading to a gate.

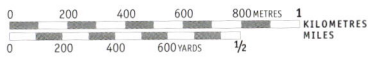

Now continue beside the wall, below broad-leaved woodland to reach another kissing-gate from which the stony path continues across a brackeny slope. When the path forks, keep right and soon you return to reach the car park at Seatoller.

●

Rydal Water and Grasmere

		GPS waypoints
Start	Grasmere	🏁 NY 339 073
Distance	5¼ miles (8.5km)	Ⓐ NY 344 068
Height gain	720 feet (220m)	Ⓑ NY 364 064
Approximate time	2¾ hours	Ⓒ NY 348 060
Parking	Stock Lane car park (Pay and Display)	
Route terrain	Fell slope paths, rocky in places; lakeshore paths; some road walking	
Ordnance Survey maps	Landranger 90 (Penrith and Keswick), Explorer OL7 (The English Lakes – South-eastern area)	

The presence of Wordsworth and his family imbue this walk with an air of poetic romance: two of his homes – Dove Cottage and Rydal Mount – are passed en route. Rydal Water is where he used to skate, the surrounding fells are those from which he drew his inspiration, Grasmere is where he lies buried, and it is certain as can be that every step of the route will have been walked by Wordsworth, too.

The first stage of the walk uses an old corpse road linking Ambleside with Grasmere, while the return to Grasmere courts the shorelines of both Rydal Water and Grasmere lake.

🏁 Set off from the Stock Lane car park, turning left and walking out to the main valley road. Cross with care and walk into the narrow road opposite that soon passes Dove Cottage.

Wordsworth moved to Dove Cottage with his sister in 1799. The cottage was formerly an inn known as the 'Dove and Olive Bough', and first recorded in a list of pubs of Westmoreland in 1617, although there is another suggestion that it did not become an inn until the second half of the 18th century, and may well have been no more than an alehouse until then: it remained a pub until 1793. Another source suggests that what became Dove Cottage was

'Built in the early seventeenth century ... previously ... an inn, known as The Dove and Olive Bough, for travellers on

the main road from Ambleside to Keswick.' In Grasmere in Wordsworth's Time, Eleanor Rawnsley describes 'The Dove and Olive Bough' as a 'house of call', namely a place, usually a public house, where journeymen connected with a particular trade assembled when out of work, ready for the call of employers; a kind of early-day job centre.

Rydal Water from the Corpse Road

Continue up the lane, ascending easily as far as a branching path on the left **A**, next to a coffin stone at the western end of a corpse road that ran, in this instance, from Ambleside to St Oswald's Church in Grasmere.

Corpse roads were a route along which the dead were transported from remote communities to places with cemeteries and burial rights, such as parish churches. Not all communities had churches, and if the dead were to be buried in consecrated ground they had to be carried across country to the nearest church. Coffin stones, such as that here, where the route leaves the lane, were places on which the coffin might be rested for a while. There would have been a number of coffin stones along the route from Ambleside, but only this one remains – what appears to be a coffin stone adjacent to a seat later on

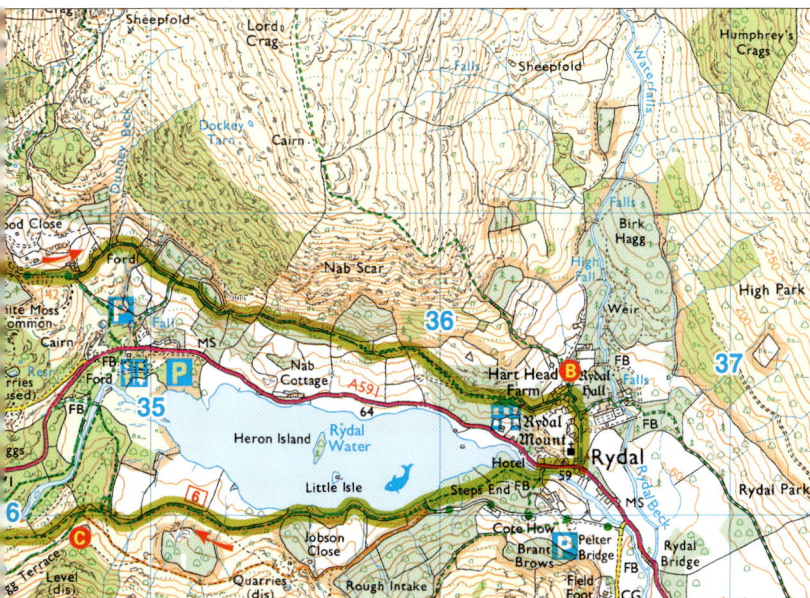

in the walk, is in fact a memorial bench.

Leave the road here, by turning left and, keeping to the right of cottages, you soon join a path climbing gently through a scattering of trees to a bench at the junction of the route going off to Alcock Tarn. Join the surfaced lane behind the bench and walk up to pass a small pond (left) and a branching track down to White Moss (right). Keep ahead on the signposted Coffin Trail.

At Dunnabeck, the road surfacing ends and the track continues between walls, soon crossing Dunney Beck. As far as Brockstone Cottage the track is surfaced with slate gravel, but here the path narrows and becomes rougher underfoot as it crosses the top of another way down to White Moss. Go forward through a bridlegate, and now enjoy a delightful traverse of the steep lower slopes of Nab Scar. The route is easy to follow, crossing pasture and woodland, and undulating gently, with fine views across Rydal Water to Loughrigg Fell. Finally, a walled section leads out to a road head, with Rydal Mount immediately to the right **B**.

Originally built in the 16th century, possibly as a yeoman's cottage, Rydal Mount was home to the Wordsworth family from 1813 until the death of Mary Wordsworth in 1859, nine years after the poet's own death. It was the largest of the Wordsworthian homes and much-loved by the family. Over the years of his residence, as Juliet Barker points out in *Wordsworth: A Life,* Rydal Mount became 'a place of pilgrimage, not just for the great and powerful in church and state, but also more touchingly, for hundreds of ordinary people who came to pay their silent tribute to his genius.'

Turn down the lane, past Rydal Mount, to reach the main valley road. Just before reaching the road, you can turn into the churchyard and pass through to a gate giving into Dora's Field. This was where Wordsworth planned to build a house when threatened with eviction from Rydal Mount. But he was allowed to stay, and he later gave the field to his daughter, Dora. It is bright in springtime with daffodils planted as a memorial to Dora, who died in 1847.

Cross the road and turn right, and a short distance farther on, bear left down to a footbridge spanning the River Rothay.

Over the bridge take the path that bears off to the right, just above the river. The path soon brings Rydal Water into view, and after a metal kissing-gate enters light woodland. Continue following the path alongside Rydal Water and then eventually climb away from it above a wall, but always following a clear, ongoing path.

With Rydal Water now behind you, the path climbs briefly along the edge of a small copse to cross a narrow ridge **C** descending from Loughrigg Fell. Keep forward, crossing the ridge, and descending towards Grasmere lakeshore. The path brings you down to a footbridge spanning the outflow from the lake. Here, keep left, walking around the edge of the lake. Keep along the lakeshore, and then soon pass through a gate into light woodland.

Stay with the shoreline path for as long as possible, until turned inland at a boat house, to take a rough path climbing to meet the Red Bank road. Now, turn right and, taking care against approaching traffic, walk towards Grasmere.

As you come into the edge of Grasmere, take the Ambleside road to a T-junction near the church. Turn right and walk past the church, then following the road (Stock Lane) which takes you back to the car park. ●

Glenridding and Lanty's Tarn

		GPS waypoints
Start	Glenridding	🥾 NY 386 169
Distance	5¼ miles (8.5km)	Ⓐ NY 379 169
Height gain	1,015 feet (310m)	Ⓑ NY 363 173
Approximate time	3 hours	Ⓒ NY 376 167
Parking	Glenridding (Pay and Display)	Ⓓ NY 381 159
Route terrain	Stony tracks; some road walking; open fellside	
Ordnance Survey maps	Landranger 90 (Penrith & Keswick), Explorer OL5 (The English Lakes – North-eastern area)	

The renown of Glenridding as one of the key tourist hotspots of the Lake District is far reaching. From here walkers launch themselves into the hills, while less energetic moments can be spent along the lakeshore or taking to one of the steamers that regularly ply up and down the lake. This was once a major mining area, and a veritable hive of industrial activity in years gone by. Taking the opportunity to visit the mining area, this walk then slips southwards into neighbouring Grisedale by way of secluded Lanty's Tarn, a spot quiet enough to attract goosander at some times of year.

🥾 Leave the main car park by walking out to the road and turning right to cross Glenridding Bridge, and then immediately right onto a narrow lane for Miresbeck and Helvellyn. Walk past a whitewashed cottage with circular chimneys typical of the Lake District, and probably dating from the late 18th century. Beyond this the lane becomes a stony track. When it forks, branch right and go towards Glenridding Beck, now following a lovely track around a camp site to emerge onto a surfaced lane at Gillside.

Turn right and cross Rattlebeck Bridge Ⓐ. The on-going lane comes out at a wider road. Go left, climbing gently and when, shortly, it forks, keep left again for Greenside Mine and Sticks Pass, to pass below rows of terraced cottages that once served the miners and their families.

The fells on your right (north) are Glenridding Dodd and Sheffield Pike, while to the south looms the massive bulk of Birkhouse Moor. The ongoing track is most agreeable and ambles up towards the main mining site. Lead ore was first discovered at what became the Greenside Lead Mine in the 1650s, the first levels being driven by Dutch adventurers in the 1690s, and dressed ore was carried to the Stoneycroft smelter at Keswick. Production at the

Eagle Cottage, Glenridding

mine, however, did not really begin until the late 18th century, and the mine was not extensively worked until 1825, when mining activity reached its height following the setting up of the Greenside Mining Company in 1822. Power was originally provided by waterwheels, with the water being supplied by the damming of nearby tarns. One of them, Keppel Cove, burst its banks on October 29, 1927, bringing disaster to the village below. Much the same happened four years later, when flood waters smashed through the concrete of High Dam.

At the height of its activity, the Greenside Mine was not only the largest lead mine in the Lake District, with over 300 employees, but was also a pioneer, being the first to use electricity to power the winding gear, and it also ran the first underground electric engine in British ore mines.

By the early 1960s it had become uneconomic to continue to extract lead from the mine, and it closed, the last ore being extracted in April 1961. But that was not entirely the end of the story for the mine was then used to test instruments designed to detect underground nuclear explosions. Most of the mine buildings are now gone, but a few remain and see service as a youth hostel and mountain huts; in fact, a bridge seat at Swart Beck is a perfect place to take a breather.

Follow the path as it ascends past the youth hostel, crosses Swart Beck and then by a waymarked route threads a group of buildings to take a waymarked track for Red Tarn and Helvellyn. The path climbs to a footbridge **B** spanning the upper reaches of Glenridding Beck, here flowing down from Keppel Cove.

Over the bridge turn left and take to the course of an old leat, which cuts an almost level path across the slopes of Birkhouse Moor. Another option takes a lower course, running along a woodland boundary and then a wall. But the leat is of admirable purpose,

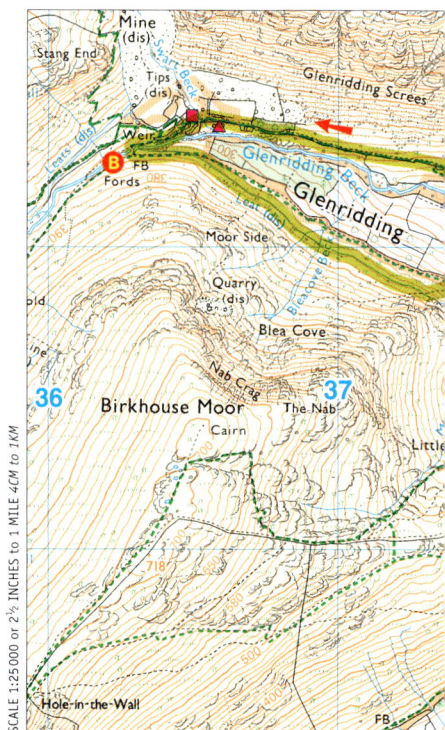

SCALE 1:25 000 or 2½ INCHES to 1 MILE 4CM to 1KM

and much preferred, finally concluding at a low wall that deflects walkers down to the lower path.

Now walk beside a wall to a ladder stile and gate **C**, where you pass onto a descending stony track that comes down to intercept a rough track serving a nearby cottage. Bear right and cross a footbridge, now taking to a path for Grisedale and Lanty's Tarn. Pass through a wall gap and then pursue a waymarked route across rough pasture.

The path leads up to a gate in a wall from which it continues, climbing easily through another gate and generally towards a shroud of trees that surround Lanty's Tarn. As you crest a rise, Lanty's Tarn comes into view, just beyond a gate. Pass to the right of the tarn, emerging on the other side to a splendid view of Grisedale. Quite who 'Lanty' of

Lanty's Tarn was, is unknown; perhaps a smuggler or illicit whisky distiller, both activities being prevalent across the Lake District in the past. The tarn is formed by a low dam, and the probability is that this was done by the Marshalls at Patterdale Hall; reputably there is an underground cellar below the dam which may well have been used as an ice house, such not being uncommon, although there is no conclusive evidence of this.

As you pass the far end of the tarn, the path drops towards Grisedale, and affords ever-improving views up this delightful valley.

Eventually you approach a couple of gates, both of which give on to the track up to Striding Edge. Take the left-hand gate **D** and then turn left down a sloping pasture to a gate at the bottom giving on to a narrow lane. Follow this across Grisedale Beck and out to a T-junction, there turning left to follow a surfaced lane down past Patterdale Hall and out to meet the main valley road.

The hall, not open to the public, is substantially rebuilt, but dates from around 1677.

Turn left at the road and cross to a path opposite, soon branching onto a path through roadside trees.

A short way farther on you pop out onto the road again. Now cross with care and continue onto a raised footpath on the opposite side, later re-crossing the road for the final stretch which will lead you back into the centre of Glenridding. ●

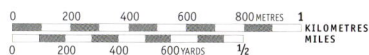

Pavey Ark and Harrison Stickle

		GPS waypoints
Start	Great Langdale, New Dungeon Ghyll	NY 294 064
Distance	4 miles (6.3km)	**A** NY 288 075
Height gain	2,300 feet (700m)	**B** NY 285 079
Approximate time	3 hours	**C** NY 278 074
Parking	Stickle Ghyll car park (NT, Pay and Display)	
Route terrain	Rough fell walking; rocky ground; steep ascent and descent	
Ordnance Survey maps	Landranger 90 (Penrith and Keswick), Explorer OL6 (The English Lakes – South-western area)	

The Langdale Pikes in profile would have been as valid an icon for the National Park Authority as that of Wasdale Head, possibly more so. They appear somewhere from almost every walk in central Lakeland included in this book, shapely, striking, seductive and hugely distinctive. Harrison Stickle is the highest of the Pikes, and its ascent gives access to other fells nearby – Loft Crag, Pike of Stickle, Thunacar Knott, Sergeant Man, High Raise, and, as embraced in this walk, Pavey Ark.

Start from the Stickle Ghyll car park in Great Langdale by walking up to the left of the buildings at the rear of the car park to follow a brief, enclosed path that leads out to a junction of paths at Stickle Ghyll. Where the track divides, bear right beside the ghyll to locate a path leading to a bridge spanning the watercourse. There has been considerable and much-needed path improvement work on the route up to Stickle Tarn, which not so long ago was in places a rock-clutching stagger. When the constructed path splits, stay with the beckside route. A small rock outcrop then has to be tackled before the path crosses the beck on boulders. Finally, nearing Stickle Tarn, the relentless uphill effort ceases and you fork right to reach the dam **A**.

The dark cliffs of Pavey Ark are inspiring and intimidating, and no place for walkers. Close observation will enable you to pick out an ascending line from the bottom right of the cliffs to near the top left. This is Jack's Rake, a breeze for some, but nonetheless a moderate rock climb and so beyond the scope of this book, although most walkers are tempted to venture into its embrace sooner or later.

For the present, cross the outlet stream to keep to the right of Stickle Tarn. Having then followed the east bank of Bright Beck for 250 yards, drop with the stony path to ford the stream. This clear but rough path now finds its way up through a breach in Pavey Ark's eastern defences. Encountering easier

SCALE 1:25000 or 2½ INCHES to 1 MILE 4CM to 1KM

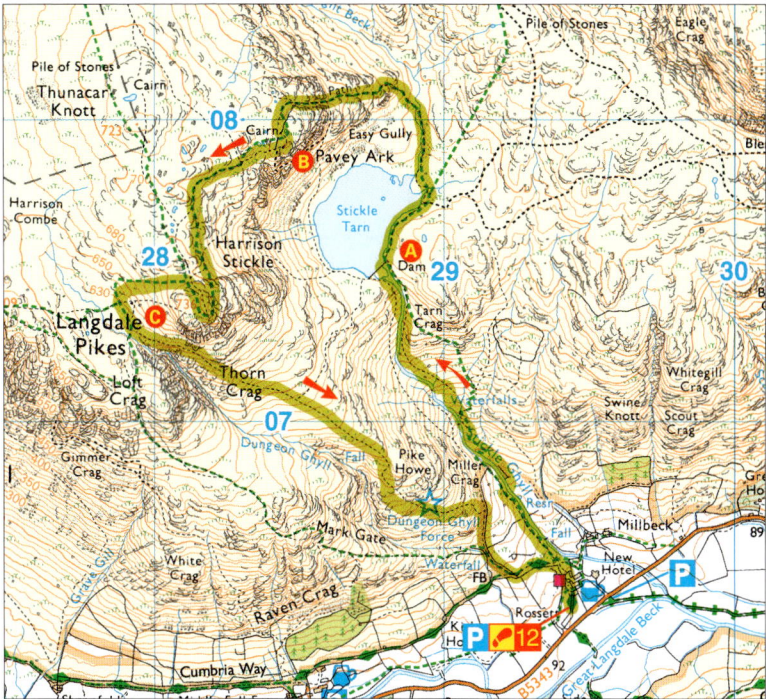

ground at the top of the rocky gully, immediately bear left, climbing a rough path to the rocky top of Pavey Ark **B**.

The onward route lies to the south-west, towards Harrison Stickle, the highest of the rocky tops along the line of high ground. It is well to get the direction firmly in mind, as many paths have materialised over the years across the intervening ground, including one ascending from the southern edge of Stickle Tarn.

Be careful not to be lured east on to this path. The best route, after initially heading south-west from Pavey Ark, heads south to cross Harrison Stickle's rugged eastern slopes before swinging west, followed quickly by a bend to the north. The summit brings respite from all uphill work and a commanding view of considerable merit.

With potentially dangerous cliffs to the south and a horrible scree path descending west from the summit, the safest way off Harrison Stickle is to set off initially in a northerly direction, as *if heading for Thunacar Knott, but then curving to the west into the boggy hollow of Harrison Combe at the top of Dungeon Ghyll* **C**.

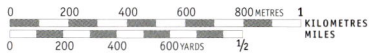

From Harrison Combe, a clear but narrow path now heads left across the upper clutches of Dungeon Ghyll. As one path crosses the beck just above the rocky ravine, stay on the north bank. With the ground on your right soon dropping away very steeply, concentration is required on the narrow path.

Once beyond the initial section, the going becomes much easier as you descend steadily towards, and then to the right of Pike Howe. The path leads down to a gate in a wall. Once through this, continue downhill with the wall on your left and then go through the next gate in it. A stony path now leads back towards Stickle Ghyll where the outward path is encountered. Bear right along this to return to the car park. ●

Dodd

Start	Mirehouse (Dodd Wood)	
Distance	4¾ miles (7.5km)	
Height gain	1,740 feet (530m)	
Approximate time	3 hours	
Parking	At start (Pay and Display)	
Route terrain	Forest trails and paths throughout	
Ordnance Survey maps	Landranger 90 (Penrith & Keswick), Explorer OL4 (The English Lakes – North-western area)	

GPS waypoints

🟨 NY 235 281
🅐 NY 235 285
🅑 NY 250 273
🅒 NY 243 269

There was a time when you couldn't see the top of Dodd for trees; now the whole summit is free of them, and the result is a rather spectacular view of Bassenthwaite and the fells beyond. For such a seemingly lowly summit on the flanks of much higher fare, Dodd is hugely popular, made more so by proximity to Mirehouse, a 17th-century house above the lake having strong associations with a number of poets, including Wordsworth, Tennyson and Southey (although this is closed during winter months).

🟨 Begin by crossing the footbridge at the rear of the **Old Sawmill Tearoom**, and then turn left onto a path that descends towards the road, but then starts to climb into the woodland, rising to a track junction at a multi-coloured waymark pole 🅐. Turn right here, and then immediately left, now climbing steadily through the forest. The path rises to another junction. Here turn right, still climbing, and following red, green and blue trails.

At the next junction, the tracks fork yet again. Here, branch left, now following the red and green trail. The path rises steadily and crosses a stream by a simple footbridge, before continuing its upwards course, although it does soon descend for a while, as the path runs on to meet a surfaced track. As it does so, turn left and follow the track high above Skill Beck.

Eventually, the path ceases to be surfaced but continues in the same direction, rising to meet a much broader trail just below the col linking

Dodd from the White Stones path

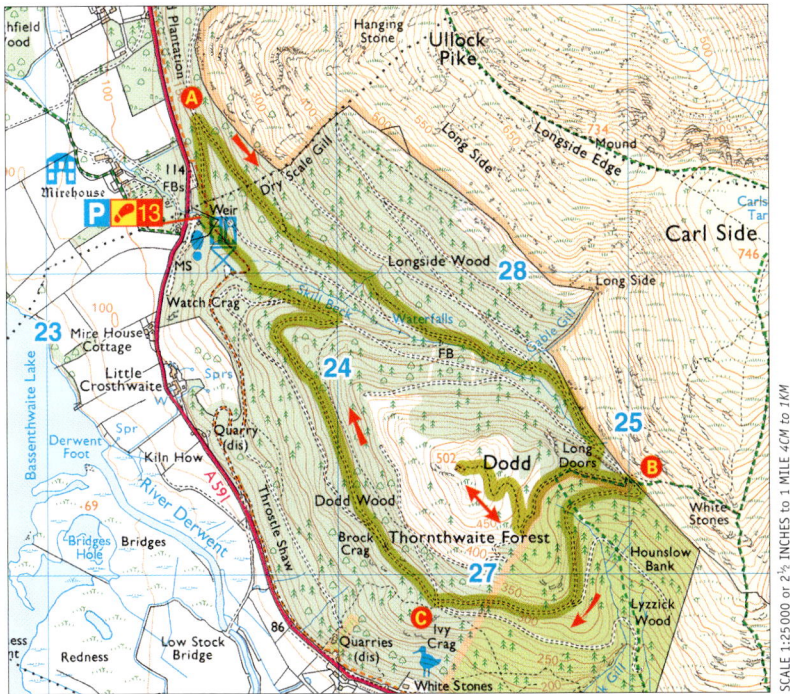

Dodd with White Stones and Carl Side. Bear right along this, and shortly ignore the track descending on the right. About 100 yards farther on you have the choice of taking a branching path up onto the summit of Dodd, which is well worth doing if the weather is clear. The summit is marked by a stone memorial pillar. Return the same way.

In the 19th century, a hermit from Scotland, by the name of George Smith, lived on Dodd. Not surprisingly, at a time when tourism was flourishing in the Lake District following the arrival of the railways, George became something of a character, known as the Skiddaw Hermit. He lived on the fell in all weathers, in a makeshift shelter of branches built against a wall. George was something of an artist, and made money by painting portraits, although some suggest his favourite sitter was any pub landlord willing to give him a drink.

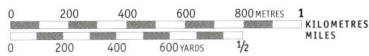

Back on the main trail, go forward across the col **B**, following the broad trail which now swings round to cross the south-eastern flank of Dodd before sweeping round the entire southern side of the fell.

Keep following the descending path, which eventually comes down to a large cleared area, a turning circle, on the left **C**. The main forest trail continues ahead; follow this.

After a spell of invigorating walking with good views across to Whinlatter Forest and the summits of Barf and Lord's Seat, the descending track finally brings you down to a track junction, where there is a signpost. Turn right onto a narrower path for Mirehouse and the tearoom. This path soon rejoins the waymarked trails and leads you down to run above Skill Beck, finally bearing left downhill beside the stream to bring you back to the start. ●

Greendale Tarn, Seatallan and Middle Fell

Greendale Tarn, Seatallan and Middle Fell

Start	Greendale	
Distance	5 miles (8km)	
Height gain	2,460 feet (750m)	
Approximate time	3½ hours	
Parking	Off-road parking at start	
Route terrain	Steep start through a rocky ravine with two fairly *steep climbs,* on to Seatallan *(optional)* and Middle Fell; *rocky descent*	
Ordnance Survey maps	Landranger 89 (West Cumbria), Explorer OL6 (The English Lakes – South-western area)	

GPS waypoints

- 🥾 NY 144 056
- Ⓐ NY 143 064
- Ⓑ NY 147 081

The craggy flanks of Buckbarrow and Middle Fell are much in evidence from the back roads around Nether Wasdale, but behind their bold front the grassy spread of Nether Wasdale Common (rising to its highest point on Seatallan) and the beautifully sited Greendale Tarn, are out of sight and seldom visited. It is the apparent shapelessness of Seatallan that perhaps deters many walkers, but this tour of Greendale, Seatallan and the adjoining minor top, Middle Fell, will be found to be one of many delights, and quite a few surprises.

🥾 From the grass and bracken beside the road at Greendale, a clear

Red Pike seen over Nether Beck

path sets off towards an obvious gully down which Greendale Gill displays a number of attractive cascades. A little steepness starts the day, but this relents a touch as a corner is rounded where you gain a better view of the gill. From the corner, a narrow path may be seen soaring upwards on to Middle Fell, and it is by this way that the walk concludes.

Meanwhile, continue along the path above the true left bank of the gill, with both the path and gill meeting at a narrowing of the ravine, a perfect place for a breather. Quite a few streams feed into the gill at this point, hence the name Tongues Gills Ⓐ.

Continue with the line of Greendale

Gill, and, as the gradient collapses completely, so the inspiring cliffs of Middle Fell come into view, opposing the gentler grassy flank of Seatallan. At any time you can cross the gill and set off up the slopes of Seatallan, but there is greater merit in continuing to Greendale Tarn, concealed until the last moment by a small morainic plug.

Though much less than an hour's walk from civilisation, beside this peaceful tarn you could be in another world. It takes a determined effort to raise yourself to cross the gill, or walk round to the northern end of the tarn and up to a broad boggy col **B** to tackle the slopes of Seatallan, although this extension is optional. There is no significant path to follow, simply an instinct for the easiest line, and this will lead you on to the vast summit plateau, at the northern end of which a trig overlooking Blengdale marks the highest point. The large mound of stones on the summit is thought to be an ancient tumulus.

From Seatallan, if you descend south of east you will come to the broad col **B** with adjoining Middle Fell, across which a path materialises, and rises through a much rockier landscape, dotted with small bright-eyed tarns, to the top of Middle Fell. The path is cairned from above the col, though it is never in doubt, and provides excellent views of the hinterland of the ancient Copeland Forest – Haycock, Scoat Fell and Red Pike, against which Scoat

Tarn and Low Tarn rest darkly.

The path continues over the top of Middle Fell, and descends through numerous rock outcrops, easily avoiding difficulties. Lower down, good views appear of the screes spilling into Wastwater from Illgill Head, against which the bright greens of the valley pastures make a vibrant contrast.

Gradually the descending path brings you back to the path corner noticed on the ascent, from where your outward steps are easily retraced. ●

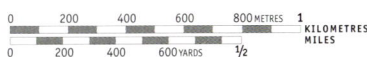

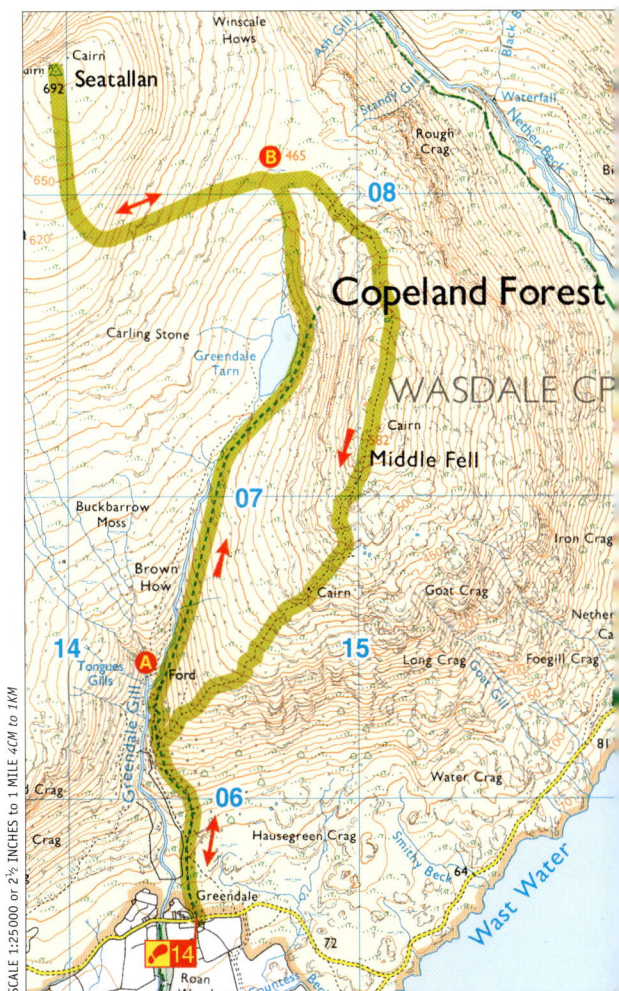

SCALE 1:25000 or 2½ INCHES to 1 MILE 4CM to 1KM

Bowscale Fell

Bowscale Fell

		GPS waypoints
Start	Mungrisdale	
Distance	5 miles (8km)	🗲 NY 364 302
Height gain	1,625 feet (495m)	Ⓐ NY 356 302
Approximate time	3 hours	Ⓑ NY 334 301
Parking	Roadside parking area (honesty payment) opposite the Village Hall	Ⓒ NY 333 305
Route terrain	Stony tracks, grassy upland, one short, steep descent	
Ordnance Survey maps	Landranger 90 (Penrith & Keswick), Explorer OL5 (The English Lakes – North-eastern area)	

Generally regarded as one of the easiest Lakeland fell summits to achieve, Bowscale Fell nevertheless involves a fair amount of ascent. In return, you achieve a splendid view into the moorland arena known as 'Back o' Skidda', a heathery, grassy wilderness that is rewarding to explore and with far fewer visitors than more central parts of the region.

The walk begins from the remote village of Mungrisdale, a tiny community where suddenly the fells give way to the lowlands of the east. The simple church of St Kentigern was built in 1756 and has a triple-decker pulpit and box pews.

🗲 Set off by crossing the bridge over the Glenderamackin and walk up to pass to the left of the **Mill Inn**, an ancient inn of Lakeland, probably 17th-century, and perfectly poised for a post-perambulatory pint or bowl of soup – it's also dog friendly. Turn right at the rear of the inn, and follow a narrow lane out to rejoin the valley road you just left. Turn left along this. A few strides farther on, branch left past the telephone box and along a broad track (signposted for Mungrisdale Common).

Directly ahead, and perhaps a little intimidating is a pyramidal fell known as The Tongue. It's actually an easterly extension of Bowscale Fell, and the

route passes easily to its left. So, go forward, following a part-stony, part-paved track until, as the Glenderamackin changes direction you can cross a footbridge over Bullfell Beck

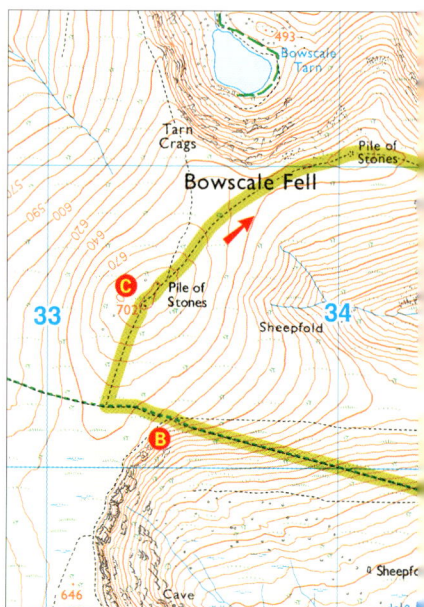

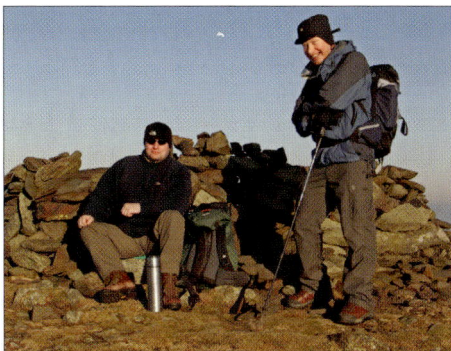

On the summit of Bowscale Fell

Ⓐ and stay along the main track, rising gently. The gradient is quite uniform, allowing frequent pauses to gaze down the valley of the Glenderamackin and across the steep eastern face of Bannerdale Crags. Keep right at two forks, always taking the higher path, which soon steepens a little as it approaches the rim of Bannerdale.

A path skims along the rim of Bannerdale, should you want to divert to include Bannerdale Crags in the walk. But then simply retrace your steps to the top of the path you have just ascended.

From the top of the ascending path, leave the rim path **Ⓑ**, by going forward across short turf on a narrow grassy path. *Off to your right, you can see the shelter on the summit of Bowscale Fell, and at any time you can make a beeline for it, crossing untracked ground.* Otherwise, for rather easier going, keep heading roughly west, and just beyond a low finger of rock you intercept another path. Here, there is a lovely view extending from Blencathra to the south, across Skiddaw to Great Calva, High Pike and Carrock Fell. At the cross path, turn right and quickly right again, heading east of north, and stroll up to the top of Bowscale Fell **Ⓒ**.

Continue across the top of the summit and head for a large cairn. Just beyond the cairn, there are two paths. A narrow grassy path descends left towards the top of unseen Tarn Crags; to the right,

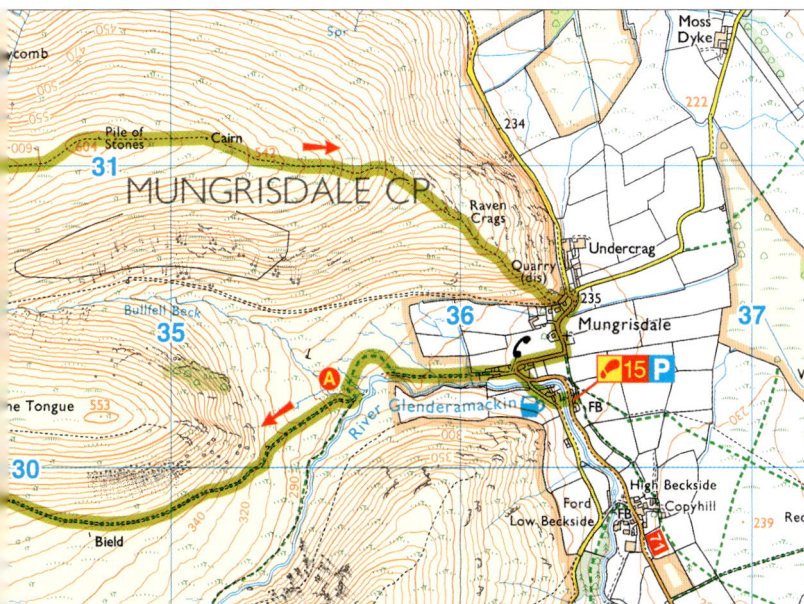

another path bears off towards the northerly arm of Bowscale Fell. Follow this soon ascending easily to large cairns on the highest ground. Unseen, below and to the left lies Bowscale Tarn, one of the most secluded tarns in Lakeland. You get a glimpse if you leave the path and walk towards the edge of the steep ground that wraps a protective arm around the tarn, *but take care not to slip here, especially in winter conditions.*

Now all that remains is to enjoy a steadily descending trek along the wide ridge. A clear path runs along the

Northwards from Bowscale Fell

highest ground, linking numerous large cairns. As you go farther east, so the route descends in a series of broad terraces, but is always clear. Eventually, at the very end of the ridge you arrive at one final steep section, where the route passes through a wide spread of gorse.

The final section is very steep, but is not unduly long, and finally, as you break free of the gorse, simply head down towards the cottages on the edge of Mungrisdale. On reaching their garden fences, turn left, through a gate and out to the valley road. Turn right and follow the road back to Mungrisdale. On the way you pass St Kentigern's Church. ●

Lord's Seat and Broom Fell

		GPS waypoints
Start	Whinlatter	
Distance	5¾ miles (9.4km)	🏁 NY 181 255
Height gain	1,755 feet (535m)	Ⓐ NY 192 260
Approximate time	3½ hours	Ⓑ NY 205 259
Parking	Spout Force car park, Whinlatter	Ⓒ NY 204 265
Route terrain	Forest trails; grassy fell summits; steep descent	Ⓓ NY 194 272
		Ⓔ NY 179 268
Ordnance Survey maps	Landranger 90 (Penrith & Keswick), Explorer OL4 (The English Lakes – North-western area)	

Lord's Seat hides itself away behind the cloak of Whinlatter Forest, but is an excellent viewpoint, easily accessible from the Whinlatter Visitor Centre, but here approached via a secluded dale and linked with grassy summits to the north-west. For the most part, the walk is hugely agreeable, but concludes with a very steep descent.

🏁 Begin from the Spout Force car park by heading along the broad forest trail that leads round into the valley of Aiken Beck, soon passing the farm at Darling How. Keep forward past a barrier, and when the trail forks, walk on along the higher track with a fine prospect ahead of Lord's Seat and the ring of grassy summits that form this remote dale.

When the track forks again Ⓐ, keep right, climbing gently across the northern slopes of Whinlatter Top. As it follows the course of Aiken Beck, the forest trail enters an area that has been cleared, and runs on along the boundary of the remaining plantation (on the left). The track climbs steadily around the cleared area and reaches a U-bend, with a rough track bearing off to the right. Ignore this and ascend a little farther to another U-bend where the main trail now clearly swings to the right and continues climbing. Here Ⓑ,

leave the forest trail, and go left onto a path through trees, that climbs directly up the head of the valley. For a time the forest closes in and you go up through a canopied tunnel of trees, before finally breaking free onto level, heather moorland.

About 200 yards along the moorland path you intercept a more substantial graded path. Turn left onto this and follow it as it leads up to a step stile Ⓒ over a fence, from which it is just a short pull onto the summit of Lord's Seat, marked by a tall pole, the remains of a fence.

Lord's Seat is the highest of the North-Western Fells and gives rise to a number of streams, all of which find their way into the River Derwent. The view is extensive, embracing the northern fells around Skiddaw, the cone of Grisedale Pike to the south, and the Galloway hills of southern Scotland beyond the Solway Firth. There are

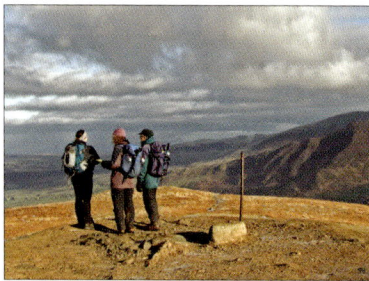

Lord's Seat summit

radiating ridges, notably east to the neat top of Barf, which can be added by strong walkers to this present route, and in a north-westerly direction, which is the way now to go.

But first you must decide if you are happy to tackle the steep descent of Graystones, which drops 920 feet (280m) in a lateral distance of 2,296 feet (700m) (less than half a mile) – 1 in 2.5 (40%). *The extension to Graystones is well worth the effort and makes the walk complete, as well as allowing you to visit Spout Force, but if you feel unable to make the descent, you need to retrace your steps from Lord's Seat. For the most part the descent from Graystones is grassy, with shale lower down; walking poles will help (if used correctly).*

Set off from Lord's Seat in a north-westerly direction. In good visibility the path is clear enough, descending as a grassy trod across moorland, but *in poor visibility it would be wise to take a moment to check the direction* because the path for Barf is rather more pronounced underfoot than that for Broom Fell.

After an initial descent, a delightful romp leads across gently swelling grassy fells, and passing through a gate/ stile in a fence beyond which lies more of the same before a final, gentle pull not so much to the summit of Broom Fell, but to a large cairn **D** and low shelter on the northern edge of the fell. (Peak baggers will need to deviate a

short distance.)

A good, grassy path now descends westwards and then south-westwards from Broom Fell before finally dropping easily to a col at the north-eastern corner of a clear-felled area of forestry. Continue above the forest boundary and over the minor top of Widow Hause; the going here is good, but northwards, in spite of excellent views, the ground spills boggily across the morass of Wythop Moss to Ling Fell.

Once beyond the clear-felled area you reach another narrow col **E**, and wall junction. Here, cross a low wooden barrier and bear right onto a steep ascending path onto Graystones. Once the brief initial ascent eases, continue roughly parallel with a wall and fence on your right, but when this bends away to the right, leave it and go forward on a clear path that leads up to a minor summit with a small cairn at NY 176 266, which is another good vantage point.

Now begins the descent, by returning the few strides to a nearby collapsed wall, and turning right beside it

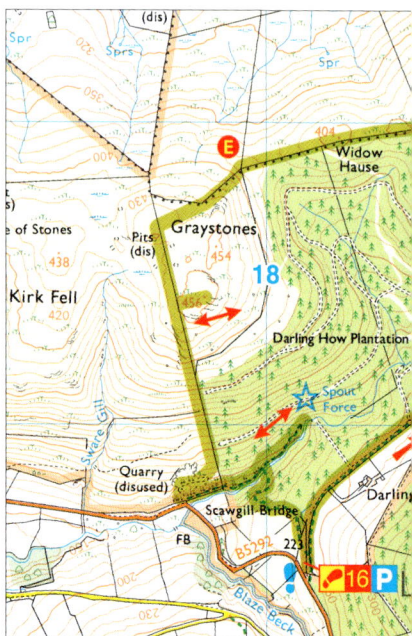

(roughly southwards), initially on an undulating path, but later starting to drop in earnest. The top of Graystones, an undistinguished mound with a small cairn, lies a little to the south-east and may be reached easily by crossing the collapsed wall, and then returning to it and the descending path a short way farther on.

The underlying rock here is from the Skiddaw Slates group, hence the smooth slopes. But you encounter large granite boulders from time to time, clearly out of place, and evidence of the handiwork of retreating glaciers, which brought the boulders (erratics) from the central area of the Lakeland fells, where the rock is volcanic.

Finally, you engage that descent, which even by strong walkers requires focus and careful placement of feet; it is mainly the steepness rather than conditions underfoot that invites caution. Alas, the view ahead is outstanding and a redeeming feature of the ascent, but should be taken in only when you are standing still.

Towards the bottom of the descent, the path runs off to the right towards Scawgill Bridge, but when it intercepts a horizontal path, turn left, soon passing through a gate beyond which a welcome seat, to the memory of Lady, awaits.

Continue along the path, now beside Aiken Beck. When you reach a footbridge, this is the way to go, although a short extension along the path leads up to Spout Force, a neat waterfall in a sheltered spot where Aiken Beck drops over a low cliff into a plunge pool. Return to the bridge.

Over the footbridge, and the next one, a narrow, stepped path climbs through a small area of cleared forest, eventually popping out onto level ground at a step stile. Cross the stile, and bear left around the edge of a pasture, initially following a fence, and then a wall, which guides you to another stile. Beyond, a short walk takes you back to the Spout Force car park. ●

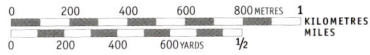

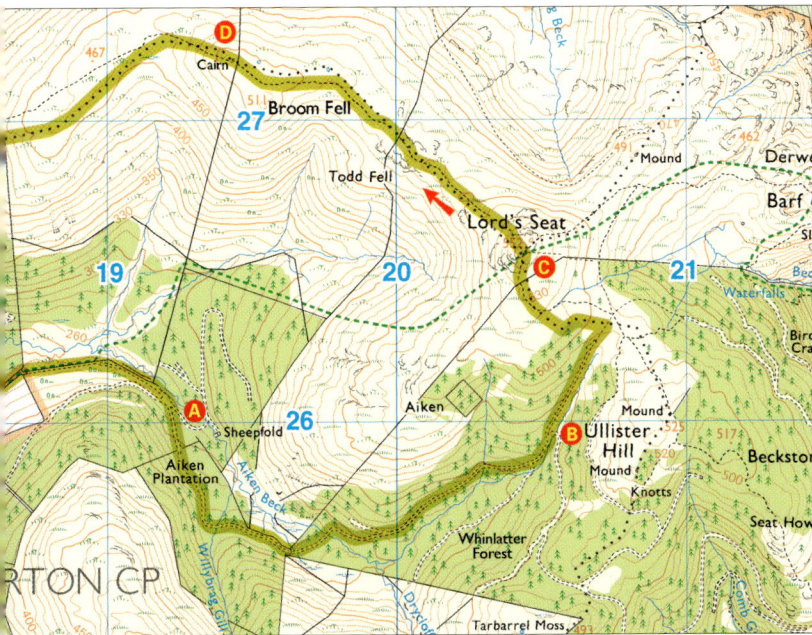

Pooley Bridge and Barton Park

		GPS waypoints
Start	Pooley Bridge	
Distance	6 miles (9.5km)	🏁 NY 469 245
Height gain	770 feet (235m)	Ⓐ NY 460 226
Approximate time	3 hours	Ⓑ NY 459 213
Parking	Pooley Bridge (Pay and Display)	Ⓒ NY 482 222
Route terrain	Lakeshore; farmland; open fell	Ⓓ NY 479 236
Ordnance Survey maps	Landranger 90 (Penrith & Keswick), Explorer OL5 (The English Lakes – North-eastern area)	

The eastern side of Ullswater, accessible from Pooley Bridge has always been a delight; relative inaccessibility lends a note of intrigue and arouses curiosity, although today visitors come in increasing numbers by steamer from Glenridding. But anyone starting this walk mid-afternoon in summer will be rewarded with a tranquility and light that is deeply satisfying. The walk touches on High Street, the Roman road, and visits an area inhabited since prehistoric times. The daffodil waymarkers of the Ullswater Way, followed for much of the time, will become a familiar sight by the end of the walk.

🏁 Begin from the Dunmallard car park at Pooley Bridge, close by the River Eamont. Cross the road bridge and on the other side turn right between gate pillars at the entrance to Eusemere Lodge.

Lined with old stone cottages and houses that exude a rustic charm, Pooley Bridge flanks the River Eamont, the former boundary between Cumberland and Westmorland. Before the first bridge was built in the 16th century, the village was simply called Pooley, a corruption of 'pool by the hill'. The hill in this case is Dunmallet – or Dunmallard, as it is known these days – which bears a small and rather undistinguished Iron Age fort.

Eusemere, south-east of the village was the home of Catherine Clarkson, the wife of anti-slavery campaigner Thomas Clarkson (1760-1846). Mrs Clarkson, referred to as such throughout her journals, was a close friend of Dorothy Wordsworth, and both Clarksons and Wordsworths spent much time together and in correspondence. (There is a memorial to Mr Clarkson set in the wall on the left soon after you reach the shore path.)

Walk along a lane for about 90 yards before turning right onto a signposted path for the lakeshore, leading to a gate. A broad track ensues, later reaching the shores of Ullswater. Continue along either the stony shore or the path above it to reach a gate near a landing stage.

The ongoing path is never far from the lakeshore and eventually reaches a camping park at Waterside House. Go forward past farm buildings, but then, just after a barrier near the campsite reception, turn left along a short access track to reach a narrow lane.

Turn right and follow the lane for about 550 yards, as far as the turning to Cross Dormont Ⓐ. Here leave the lane and turn left up the access track. Just before reaching the farm buildings, bear right to a pair of gates. Go through,

swing up to the left to another gate, and then continue straight on to yet another and a waymark by the edge of a caravan site.

Go through the gate and continue beside a fence to a pair of gates near the end of a low farm building. Go through the small gate in the wall to the right of the building and walk with the wall on your left. When the wall then bends left,

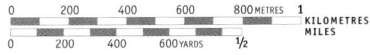

Ullswater, near Pooley Bridge

keep straight on, through yet another gate. On the far side of the field, a wooden gate gives onto a continuing path beside a wall, which later swings left. Cross a narrow beck to a gate and, in the ensuing field, maintain the same direction to the right of a barn at Crook-a-dyke Farm. Now keep forward on a vehicle track for Howtown and Martindale.

As the track bears right towards Thwaitehill Farm, leave it by turning towards a gate in the intake wall, which gives onto a path through rough pasture. This leads through a broad spread of gorse, after which a narrower trail to the left is ignored. Another junction is soon reached. Ignoring one trail to the right here, follow the main path left and, almost immediately, take another trail on the right. This climbs easily towards Auterstone Wood and then intercepts a broad track **B** at the base of Barton Fell, which soars steeply above the route.

Turn left along the track, which climbs steadily and then levels as it approaches the top edge of more woodland, Barton Park. Continue on a clear path above the top edge of the woodland. Beyond the woods, bear right at a fork, dropping into a shallow ravine containing Aik Beck.

After crossing Aik Beck, the clear track presses on across open moorland, heading towards the low dome of Heughscar Hill. The track later crosses the route of the Roman road, High Street, linking the forts at Ambleside and Brougham.

Beyond the head of another stream, Elder Beck, the track reaches the edge of a low stone circle, known as The Cockpit **C**. Little is known about The Cockpit. As a stone circle it is not especially impressive, although it is actually a concentric ring. The date is unknown, but probably Bronze Age like the numerous barrows and cairns dotted about the top of adjacent Askham Fell. The name suggests that the site may well have been used in the past as an arena for fighting cocks, but it is unlikely that it would have been built for this purpose.

From The Cockpit, follow the track as it bears left (ignore the paths to the right). This leads on to intercept another track at a large cairn, just below Heughscar Hill, having followed the Roman road for a short distance. But at the cairn, leave this ancient highway by turning left onto a very broad track that descends easily above the northern reaches of Ullswater to reach the top end of a surfaced lane at Roehead **D**.

Now simply follow the lane downwards to return to Pooley Bridge. Go straight over at the crossroads and left at the mini-roundabout to reach the bridge once more, turning right to return to the car park. ●

Tarn Hows

Start	Hawkshead
Distance	6 miles (9.5km)
Height gain	985 feet (300m)
Approximate time	3¼ hours
Parking	Hawkshead (Pay and Display)
Route terrain	Farmland; woodland; fell tracks; some road walking
Ordnance Survey maps	Landranger 90 (Penrith & Keswick) and 97 (Kendal & Morecambe), Explorer OL7 (The English Lakes – South-eastern area)

GPS waypoints

- ✔ SD 354 980
- Ⓐ SD 335 990
- Ⓑ SD 327 998
- Ⓒ NY 331 007
- Ⓓ SD 342 994
- Ⓔ SD 350 986

Hawkshead is laden with Wordsworth and Beatrix Potter memorabilia, and as a result has become a tourist-saturated hot spot at certain times of year. Yet without these literary associations, Hawkshead would still attract visitors for its splendid architecture, its lovely setting, ancient pubs and an air of tranquility. Not far away lies Tarn Hows, another popular tourist destination, so linking the two, as this walk does, is both logical and attractive. Out of season the area is quieter, but you are never likely to tackle this walk without company somewhere in sight.

Chapel, Hawkshead Hill

📝 Turn left out of the car park and, with the Grammar School attended by Wordsworth directly ahead, veer right into the main part of the village. Keep straight ahead, passing to the left of the **Queen's Head** on a pedestrian walkway. On your right in a short while are the offices once used by Beatrix Potter's husband, William Heelis, a local solicitor.

Turn left, passing to the rear of the **Kings Arms Hotel**, and going into Vicarage Lane. You soon pass Ann Tyson's cottage, where Wordsworth boarded. Now follow the ongoing lane out of Hawkshead and continue to a footpath on the right, signposted for Tarn Hows. Turn through the gate here and follow a path across a pasture, and up to a gate. Go forward towards and along the edge of mixed woodland.

Shortly the path runs alongside a stream, which it crosses by a footbridge, after which it scampers rockily up to a gate at the top edge of the woodland. A path now leads on across a large pasture, crosses a concrete farm track, and eventually comes down to meet a road near Hawkshead Hill.

Turn left along the road, walk into the village and then take the first lane on the right (just after the chapel). Ignoring a turning for Ambleside on the right, continue to a T-junction. Go left and immediately right along a narrow lane for Tarn Hows. Shortly, leave the lane through a kissing-gate on the left **Ⓐ**. Follow a continuing path above the road, quickly forking right to cross a tiny beck. The path crosses two bracken-filled pastures, climbing steadily. On the far side of the second field, go through the right-hand one of two kissing-gates to enter an area of light broadleaved woodland.

The path climbs steadily through the woodland, never far from the road to Tarn Hows which, at one point it almost rejoins, but instead descends into a stand of mature conifers. The path does finally come back out onto the road, where Tarn Hows now eases into view. Bear left down the road for a short distance until you can take a clear grassy path going off on the right towards the tarn.

The path comes down to intercept a broad surfaced track that circles around the tarn. Turn left on this and then fork right to walk above the southern edge of the tarn. Pass through a gate and across the top of the path ascending via Tom Gill **Ⓑ**. Keep on along the western tarnside path, at varying distances from it until, as you approach the northern end of the tarn, leave the main path, and branch left at a signpost for Skelwith Bridge and the Langdales. This path cuts through light woodland, mainly birch, below Tom Heights.

The path ends at a kissing-gate where it gives on to a broad stony track **Ⓒ**. Turn right for Iron Keld and Hawkshead.

The trail is a Byway Open to All Traffic, so take care against vehicles, usually motor bikes that use it from time to time. The track climbs at first, but soon levels and sets off in splendid fashion across hummocky terrain. Once beyond the turning into the Iron Keld Plantation the track starts to descend and provides lovely forward views embracing quite a panorama from Esthwaite Water, across Claife Heights and Latterbarrow, to the distant Howgills, the low fells beyond Windermere, Wansfell set against the Kentmere Fells, Stony Cove Pike and Red Screes above Kirkstone and Little Hart Crag, at the head of Scandale, tucked in between Red Screes and the eastern arm of the Fairfield Horseshoe.

Nearing Borwick Lodge, keep right as a rough track drops left. On reaching the road, turn right and immediately left along the side lane for Hawkshead

D, taking care against approaching traffic on this narrow lane. The lane descends to intercept a road. Turn left and take particular note of the architecture of the cottages nearby, which have large circular chimneys, and the curious stone-built structure off to the left, which is the Hawkshead Courthouse.

Hawkshead Courthouse is all that remains of a medieval farm that belonged to Furness Abbey until the Dissolution of the Monasteries in 1537. Hawkshead Hall Farm, formerly Hawkshead Old Hall, was part of the monastic grange.

The road comes down to meet the B5286. Turn right, and then at Keen Ground Lodge leave the road for a driveway on the right **E** for Walker Ground. As you reach the entrance to Keen Ground, go left through a gate and immediately right to two waymarks. From the second of these, bear diagonally left across a hummocky pasture to a gate and kissing-gate from which an indistinct grassy path cuts across the slope of another field, to a step stile (with dog gate). Cross this to intercept the outward route. Here turn left beside a fence in order to retrace your steps back to Hawkshead village. ●

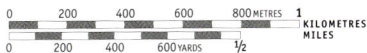

Dent and Kinniside Stone Circle

		GPS waypoints
Start	Cleator Moor	
Distance	7 miles (11km)	NY 030 144
Height gain	1,575 feet (480m)	Ⓐ NY 023 134
Approximate time	4 hours	Ⓑ NY 027 135
Parking	Roadside parking at Wath Bridge	Ⓒ NY 055 130
Route terrain	Open fell tops and tracks; woodland tracks	Ⓓ NY 057 139
Ordnance Survey maps	Landranger 89 (West Cumbria), Explorer OL4 (The English Lakes – North-western area)	

The fell is a superb vantage point, showing what lies ahead for long-distance walkers on the Coast-to-Coast Walk with a come-hither-if-you-dare challenge that will unsettle a few. Closer to hand, lies one of the last unsung dales of Lakeland, Uldale. This walk takes a glimpse into the dale, before strolling through Nannycatch and up onto Blakeley Moss where there is a stone circle.

The key to the walk is the small town of Cleator Moor, historically linked with the iron works industry; the influx of Irish workers gave the town the nickname 'Little Ireland'. On the outskirts of town lies Wath Bridge – 'wath' being a Scandinavian word for a ford or crossing point. Today, there is a fine bridge, spanning the River Ehen, which has its source in Ennerdale Water.

Start from the nearby roadside parking and cross the bridge, turning immediately right onto a narrow side lane. You follow this lane, with good views to the west, towards the coast, for one mile, as far as Black How Plantation on the left Ⓐ, opposite a group of cottages. Here, leave the road and turn into the plantation, taking to a broad, gravel track rising into woodland. When you reach a junction Ⓑ, turn left for Dent Fell, and now following a

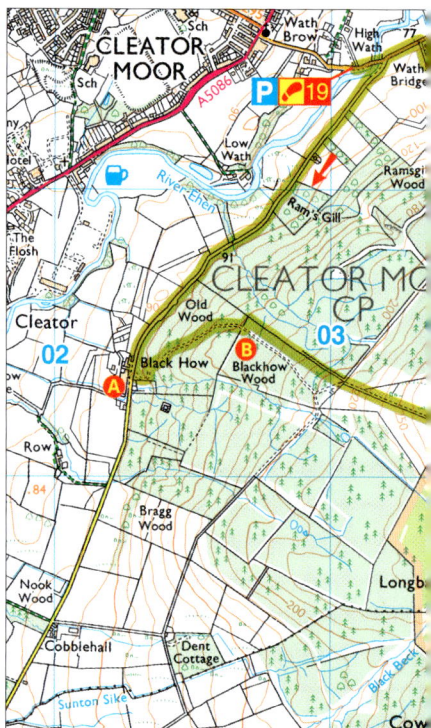

Kinniside Stone Circle

narrow path along the edge of a larch plantation. After about 100 yards, the path swings to the right, and climbs through a firebreak towards Dent Fell.

At the top of the plantation, cross a track, and go forward beside a fence, maintaining this direction onto the highest part of the fell. Optimism may lead you to hope that the prominent cairn you see ahead is the top of the fell. But reality shows it to be a shelter, with the very modest cairn that marks the true summit another 600 yards distant

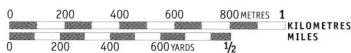

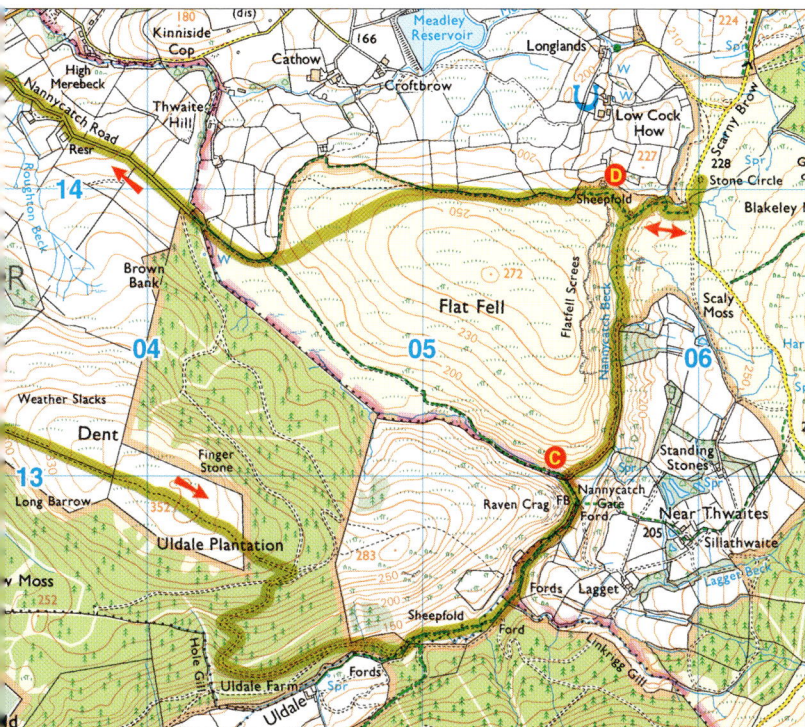

SCALE 1:26316 or 2½ INCHES to 1 MILE 3.8CM to 1KM

Wath Bridge, Cleator Moor

across a grassy summit plateau.

Just a few strides beyond the cairn, the path starts to descend. Cross a stile, and continue down through an area of cleared plantation to intercept a forest trail. Turn right, and shortly meet another track. Cross this and go down along the edge of the plantation, with more cleared areas to the right. The descending track is steep in places, and requires care, but you get lovely cameos of Uldale framed by trees.

Eventually, the track merges with another running out from Uldale. Go forward along this to another junction, and here turn left, almost immediately leaving the broad trail for a bridleway on the left, passing through a gate, and then following a charming route through a simple dale, crossing and recrossing a stream in the process.

Follow the path until it reaches a gate and stile ● (known as Nannycatch Gate), beyond which the path divides. Turn right, keeping east of Flat Fell, and when, just after crossing a small stream, the path divides, bear right past a low hillock. The path climbs towards the moorland road, but when it forks bear sharp right to go up to the road. The Kinniside Stone Circle lies a short distance to the

left, on the other side of the road.

Kinniside Stone Circle may be a bit of a sham, a modern creation, but one that is probably on or near the site of a prehistoric circle. A number of the original stones, were long ago taken for farming use, but in 1925 a restoration job was carried out by a Dr Quinn, using many of the original stones, which had been tracked down, recovered and set in concrete.

Having visited the stone circle, retrace your steps into Nannycatch Valley, but as you go back, instead of taking a lower path used earlier, stay on a slightly higher path ● that curves round to the right into a western arm of the dale and feeds into a broad track, initially cobbled, and leading up onto the north side of Flat Fell.

The path accompanies a wall for some distance and then as both wall and path start to descend as you draw level with the western end of Meadley Reservoir to the north, move away from the wall, bearing left across the slope of Flat Fell. The path brings you down to the top end of Nannycatch Road, here a rough track. Turn right onto it; after a gate the road becomes surfaced and leads down to emerge on the valley road a short distance north east of Wath Bridge, and the completion of the walk. ●

Ennerdale

		GPS waypoints
Start	Ennerdale Bridge	🖊 NY 085 154
Distance	7 miles (11.5km)	Ⓐ NY 131 138
Height gain	655 feet (200m)	Ⓑ NY 112 151
Approximate time	3½ hours	Ⓒ NY 090 158
Parking	Two car parks at Broadmoor	
Route terrain	Lakeside paths; forest trails	
Ordnance Survey maps	Landranger 89 (West Cumbria), Explorer OL4 (The English Lakes – North-western area)	

In spite of a long-standing reputation as a depressing place, 'claustrophobically blanketed' in dark pines, the long valley of Ennerdale is at last beginning to see the light. The cloak of trees, for so long the object of criticism, has been thinned and cleared. Walks have been introduced through and around the valley that appeal to walkers of all standards, and, still in the early stages of its eastbound journey, the Coast-to-Coast Walk, renowned for its discerning quality, passes down the length of the valley before crossing to Honister Pass and Borrowdale.

At the head of the dale, Pillar dominates, with Steeple close by, always peering across the expanse of the lake, or as mountain cameos through gaps in the trees. But best of all, there is no unauthorised vehicular access beyond Bowness Knott, the dale is the preserve of pedestrians only, and all the better for it.

🖊 The walk begins from a car park near the western end of the lake, and about a mile east of Ennerdale Bridge. Go left after the car park, and follow a broad track to the foot of Ennerdale Water. Here, turn right along the southern shore of the lake. Arrival at the edge of this substantial lake, across which the swelling sides of Great Borne and Starling Dodd soar bulkily upwards, is an inspiring moment.

Things have changed in Ennerdale Bridge since one traveller described the pub as 'small, dirty, and filled with roaring tipplers' – and that at nine in the morning! The village now sees few visitors, its general inaccessibility ensuring that the throngs do not stumble upon it other than inadvertently. Thankfully, it remains a quiet farming and forestry retreat, well known and loved by local people, but never likely to figure highly on tourist itineraries.

In prehistoric times, iron was smelted here, and much later haematite was mined along the valley of Ennerdale. There were also a number of small industries here related to weaving, and Ennerdale Bridge grew as a result.

Ennerdale Water

SCALE 1:25000 or 2½ INCHES to 1 MILE 4CM to 1KM

A good path skirts the lake's shore, never far from the water until it encounters the rocky thrust of Angler's Crag. Strong walkers can leave the path a little before Angler's Crag and clamber over its summit for a splendid view of the valley, and a long steady descent to rejoin the lower path.

There is no denying the beauty of Ennerdale. Edwin Waugh, a notable Lancashire poet, and at his best when revelling in the wild and stormy side of nature, wrote a most evocative description of the lake in his *Rambles in the Lake Country*. Of a moonlit visit he penned: 'In this sheltered corner little eddies of shimmering silver flit about — the dainty Ariels of moonlit water; there, is a burnished islet of stirless brilliance, in which even the moon smiles to see herself look so passing fair; and, out beyond, the wide waters are in a tremulous fever of delight with her sweet influence ... If there be magic in the world, it is this!'

A less demanding option continues at a lower level, through the fractured base of the crag. Close by, a small headland jutting into the lake, is known as Robin Hood's Chair, though there is scant evidence that this legendary hero ever

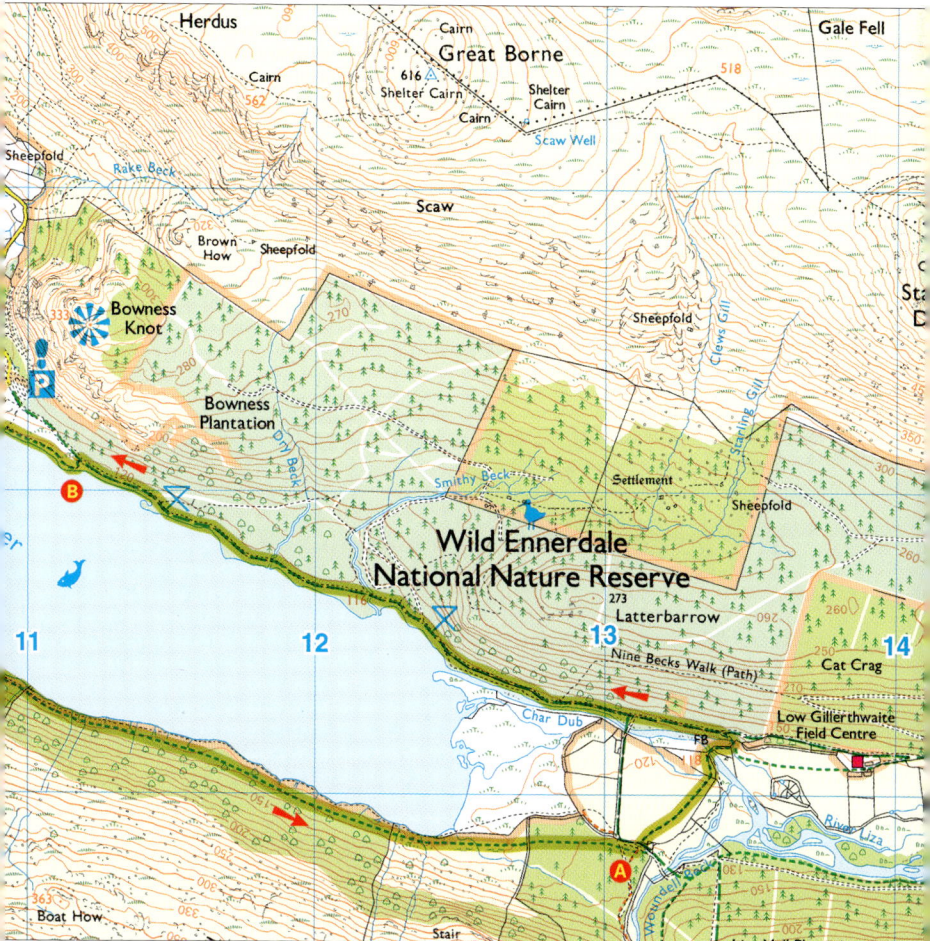

The village of Ennerdale Bridge, with Broadmoor woodland and Ennerdale Water beyond

ventured this far. Even so, it's a significant moment for Coast-to-Coasters, as they're all heading for Robin Hood's Bay.

Once beyond Angler's Crag, the path continues pleasantly to the head of the lake, where a path **A** sweeps round to join the main valley trail at Irish Bridge (not named on maps). Turn left onto the broad trail and enjoy easy-going walking on this bridleway for the next

Ennerdale and Pillar

1½ miles (2.4km).

Before reaching the Bowness Knott car park, a path **B** leaves the main trail to go down to the lakeshore, which should now be followed all the way around the northern loop of the lake to a point **C** where a path runs westward to Broadmoor woodland. Ignore this and stay on a clear path, still following the lake shoreline and shortly cross the lake outflow at a weir. Then turn right, retracing your outward steps to return to the starting point. ●

Wast Water

		GPS waypoints	
Start	Wasdale	📷	NY 151 054
Distance	8 miles (12.5km)	🅐	NY 148 048
Height gain	740 feet (225m)	🅑	NY 142 039
Approximate time	4 hours	🅒	NY 152 045
Parking	Numerous roadside parking areas and car parks		
Route terrain	Woodland paths; rugged and uneven tracks across boulder slopes; road walking		
Ordnance Survey maps	Landranger 89 (West Cumbria), Explorer OL6 (The English Lakes – South-western area)		

The remoteness of Wasdale is acutely inspirational: a heady tang of wild, uncut mountain gems that soar from valley sides with the air of majesty. Towards the head of the dale rise Yewbarrow, Great Gable and Lingmell, an iconic trio that compose the emblem of the Lake District National Park. With this assembly almost always in view, this walk takes a tour of the valley's lake, Wast Water, and offers the extremes of easy roadside walking in a superb setting and the most rugged test of footwear, balance and nerve across the infamous Wasdale screes.

There are numerous parking places along the length of Wasdale, some simple roadside pull-ins, others 'Pay and Display' or 'Honesty Box' parking areas. Where you start is irrelevant; it all depends on whether you want your road walking at the start or the end of your walk.

📷 Set off in a south-westerly direction along the road, following it until, as it approaches the grounds of Wasdale Hall (now a youth hostel, and originally built in 1829), it swings to the right, away from the lake. Here, leave the road and locate a ladder stile 🅐 giving into light woodland, through which you follow a lakeside path towards the youth hostel. On the way, the path passes a perfectly placed bench from which to admire the view up the

valley – on some days you may go no farther; it's all quite idyllic.

Beyond the youth hostel the lakeside path makes a loop around Low Wood, a small wooded hill, to reach a boat house, where the path now swings to the right in order to find a way that takes you to the building on the opposite shore; it's actually a pumping station.

When the path forks, bear left, and gradually you pass the end of the lake and take to the River Irt that flows from it (always a good quiz question). Eventually the path comes to a kissing-gate in a wall, just by Lund Bridge 🅑. Cross the bridge and follow a path going to the left to reach a service track to the pumping station. Turn left along this, and when you reach the building, keep to the right of it to begin the

Copeland Forest

WASDALE CP

Carling Stone

Greendale
Tarn

Cairn

Middle Fell

07

Buckbarrow
Moss

Brown
How

Cairn

Goat Crag

Iron Crag

Waterfall

Bowderdale

Stone
Pillar

Overbeck Bridge

P

Ford

Netherbeck Bridge
Cattle Grid

Foegill Crag

Landing
Stage

Long Crag

Tongues
Gills

d Crag

l Crag

Hausegreen Crag

Greendale

Water Crag

06

81

Wast Water

14

15

72

FB
Roan
Wood

Countess Beck

21

16

Low Iron Cra

High Iron Crag

Cattle Grid

High
Birkhow

Wasdale
Hall

81

05

Vicker's How

Low
Adam Crag

Bell Rib

Cam

Cairn

Illgill He

derdale
Beck

The
Lodge

C

A

High
Adam Crag

The Screes

Broken Rib

B

Low Wood

Lund
Bridge

Bell Crag

04

Broad
Crag

Little Gram Gill

River Irt

Pens End

Cairn

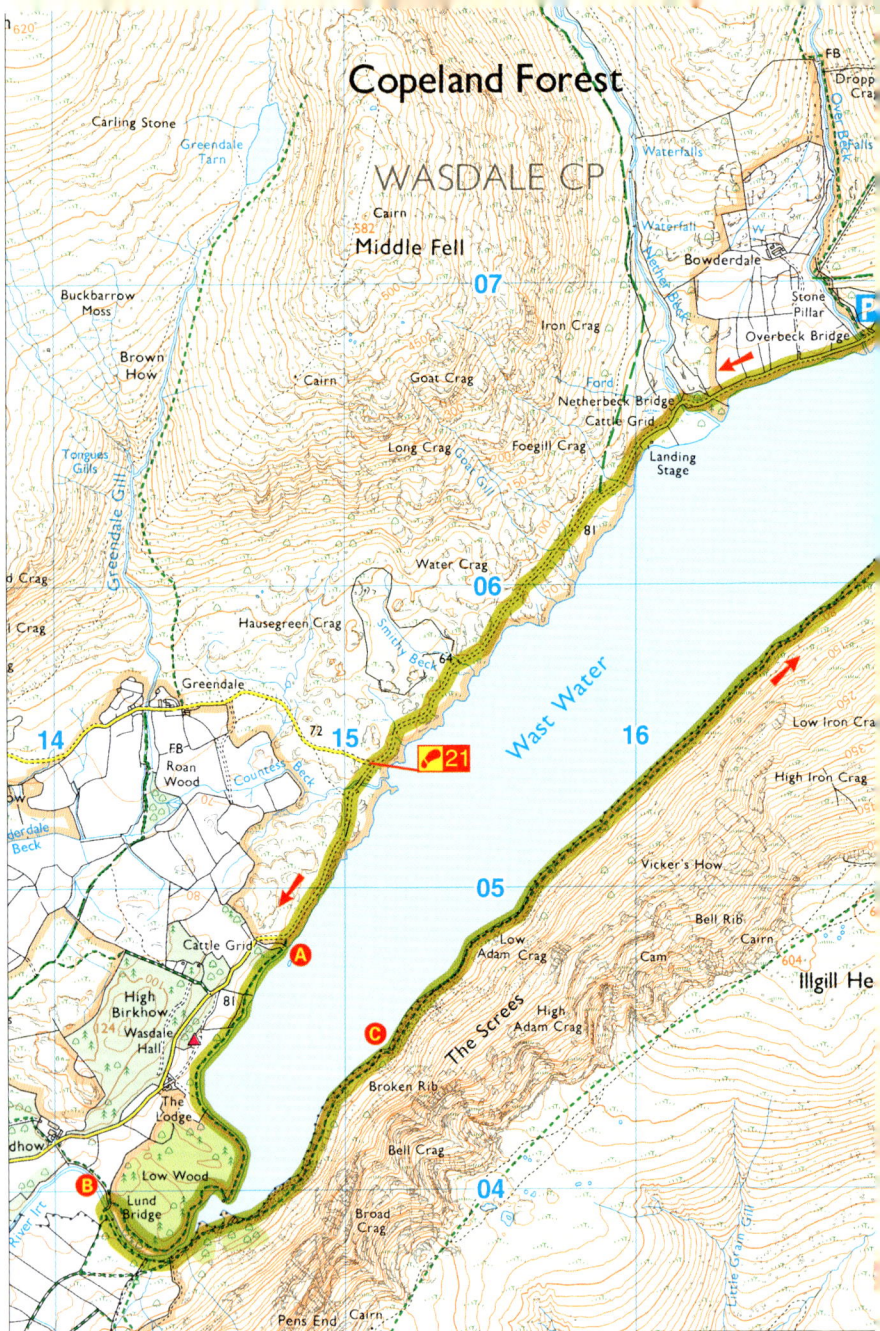

traverse of Wast Water screes, which
sets off as a narrow path.

Now is a good time to take in
Wasdale. The lake is almost 3 miles
(4.5km) long, and ½ mile wide (800m);
it lies 215 feet (65m) above sea level,
but the bottom of the lake is more than
230 feet (70m) down – below sea level.

This is one of the finest examples of a
glacially over-deepened valley. The
steep slopes on the south-eastern side of
the lake rise to the summits of Illgill
Head and Whin Rigg, perfectly
innocuous summits in their own right
viewed from the south, but with a
downfall of scree that is awesome. The

Scale bar:
0 200 400 600 800 METRES 1 KILOMETRES
0 200 400 600 YARDS ½ MILES

yards above the water's edge, and to try as much as possible to maintain the same direction. If you arrive on the other side directly on the continuing path, you have done very well.

Once beyond the first main downfall, a path does then lead on. Subsequent downfalls are of smaller boulders, and a path becomes possible. After all the screes have been passed, a simple path leads out to Wasdale Head Hall Farm, and then Brackenclose, before finally crossing Lingmell Gill and the wider Lingmell Beck, where new bridge works have become necessary to accommodate the seasonal effects of this important water course. Three bridges have come and gone in the last 100 years at this point, necessitating the development of a river naturalisation scheme that will see bridge development work undertaken.

Over Lingmell Beck, you soon reach the valley road, and all that remains is to turn left and walk back to your starting point. ●

Wast Water and the screes

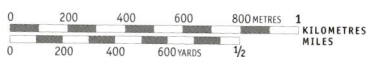

screes, which you are about to tread, were formed as a result of ice and erosion, and rise for over almost 2,000 feet (600m).

The scree has, however, been in situ for many, many years, and has amply stabilised. But it is vital to ensure the correct placement of feet, and not attempt to rush across. The larger boulders are more 'fixed' than the smaller, but as you cross the screes, an exhilarating experience, it is important that you relax and take your time. It is all very special: mildly intimidating, exhilarating, enthralling, energizing, thrilling and distinctly unique.

When you reach the first major downfall of scree ⑥, the path disappears: the boulders are large, and it is impossible for a path to be fashioned across them. The key is to keep between 10–15

St Bees Head

St Bees Head

		GPS waypoints
Start	St Bees	NX 961 117
Distance	8 miles (12km)	**A** NX 949 151
Height gain	1,215 feet (370m)	**B** NX 968 149
Approximate time	4¼ hours	**C** NX 981 141
Parking	Beach promenade (Pay and Display)	
Route terrain	Cliff-top path (Cumbria Coastal Way); lanes and field paths	
Ordnance Survey maps	Landranger 89 (West Cumbria), Explorer 303 (Whitehaven & Workington)	

The sea cliffs of St Bees are a fabulous viewpoint with especial appeal for birdwatchers. Coincidentally, St Bees is the starting (or finishing point) of the Coast-to-Coast Walk, which jaunts across the breadth of Britain to Robin Hood's Bay on the Yorkshire coast. The walk uses the 'C2C', as it is referred to, for the greater part of the route, but then bids it farewell as it makes an agreeable return to St Bees.

Set off by walking past the Lifeboat Station and on reaching the foreshore turn right around the edge of a caravan site to locate a footbridge giving onto a path rising onto South Head, also known as Tomlin. Not surprisingly, given the wealth of birdlife that appears (and breeds) along the sea cliffs in the course of a year, the whole area is an RSPB Nature Reserve.

The history of St Bees is fascinating and extensive. The village is said to owe

St Bees South Head

Map labels (as visible on the map):

Quarry Bungalows
Quarry (dis)
A
15
Sandwith
126
Croftfoot
P
Tarnflatt Hall
Hannahmoor Lane
North Head
St Bees Lighthouse
117
Sandwith Newtown
Cloven Barth
Hannah Moor
14
High House
Poultr Farm
94
95
96
Fleswick
141
Rottington
St Bees Head
31
Rottington Hall
13
FBs
Cumbria Coastal Way
Rottington Cottages
Tomlin
Christy Meadow Bridge
Scale
Rottington Beck
Sheepfold
110
South Head
12
Gutter Foot
FB
IRB Sta
Sch
Eaglesfield
Pattering Holes
P
22
Peckmill Hotel
P

SCALE 1:25000 or 2½ INCHES to 1 MILE 4CM to 1KM

0 200 400 600 800 METRES 1
                              KILOMETRES
                              MILES
0 200 400 600 YARDS ½

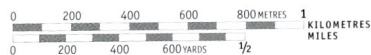

its name to Bega, a 7th-century saint cast ashore at Fleswick Bay. The earliest records about St Bega come from the *Life and Miracles of St Bega the Virgin*, a manuscript now in the British Museum, and dating from the 12th century.

Tradition has it that on the day that Bega, the daughter of an Irish king, was supposed to be married to a Norse prince, she fled the court, and was transported by an angel to the Cumbrian coast. Here, recovered from her journey, she asked the local lord for

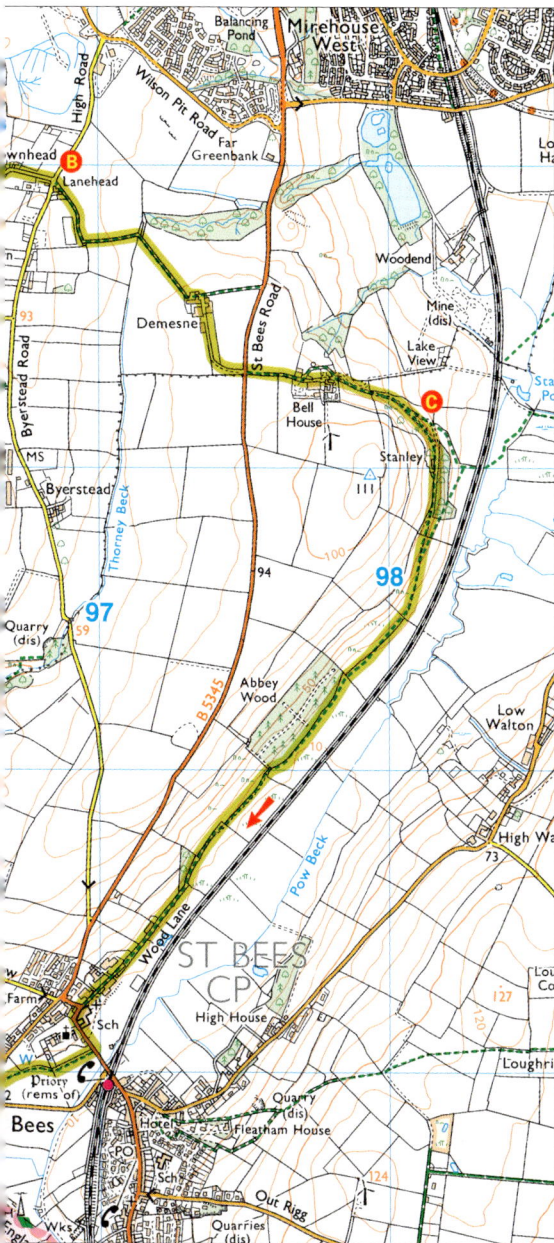

her the land and she went on to found a small nunnery that in time grew to become the powerful Priory of St Bees.

Present-day St Bees was not always so named. In the Henry VIII's *Valor Ecclesiasticus* of 1535, the village is identified as Kyrkeby Becok. When the priory was dissolved in 1539, the translation of its Latin name rendered it as the cell of St Bees. And St Bees it has been ever since.

The path across South Head is clear, *but does stray close to the sea cliffs in a way that may intimidate anyone without a head for heights*. To make things easier, you will find a couple of places where kissing-gates have been introduced into boundary fences to enable a route to be made that does not venture too close to the edge. In reality, the 'new' routes thus opened up are simply following the collapsed and largely buried course of ancient field boundaries.

land on which to build a nunnery. He replied dismissively that she could have as much land as was covered the next day by snow. He probably thought, it being midsummer at the time, that he had seen the last of the woman. But miracles happen, and the next day it snowed. The lord, true to his word, gave

Along much of the route, gorse is abundant, imbuing the air with the heady scent of cinnamon. An old Second World War lookout station, built in 1938 and manned throughout the war, today invites a welcome breather.

The first indent to the clifftop route

Lighthouse, St Bees Head

comes at Fleswick Bay, where you turn briefly inland to cross a ravine, and continue to climb onto North Head, adorned by a lighthouse. Here the path keeps to the landward side of a fence, again following the course of an old field boundary.

Continue past the lighthouse to find that the route takes a north-easterly direction, with Whitehaven now in view across Saltom Bay. Not long after passing a welcome bench, you also pass an old step stile **A**. Ignore this, and keep around the edge of a field, heading towards a nearby wall gap. Now keep the gorse-covered wall on your left and walk up-field to intercept a vehicle track that soon runs on between hedges to emerge on a lane close by a conspicuous radio mast.

Turn left and follow the lane down to the village of Sandwith. As you enter the village, turn left, walk past the **Dog and Partridge** pub, and continue along the lane to a T-junction at Lanehead **B**. Cross the road and go into the lane opposite (signposted for St Bees road via Demesne). The lane soon becomes a narrow path between hedgerows.

When you reach Demesne, swing left into the farmyard, and then turn right onto a Coast-to-Coast footpath that runs between farm buildings and out along a broad track to reach the St Bees road. Cross the road and go down the lane opposite to Bell House and Woodside. After the buildings, the track descends to cross a cattle grid. Shortly, when the track forks, keep right to reach a gate after which the track starts to descend. At a low waymark **C**, the Coast-to-Coast takes its leave, descending left to a gate. Now simply keep on with the main track to pass Stanley Farm, and continue on a broad track.

Follow the ongoing track as far as a waymark where it turns left to go down to a railway crossing. Here leave the track and keep on in the same direction. The way is pathless, but follows the course of an old wall that will guide you to two stiles at the bottom corner of distant Abbey Wood.

Cross the stiles and continue at the top edge of a rough pasture, walking parallel with the woodland boundary. On the far side of the wood, pass through a makeshift sheep enclosure and press on along a broad track beyond. This runs on to a kissing-gate giving into a large car park adjoining St Bees School. Walk past the school buildings and out to meet a road. Turn left and walk down towards St Bees centre. Just on passing the priory church, turn right onto a signposted path that runs across fields towards the coast.

On the far side, the path makes two escapes from the field. On the right, steps lead up to a gate giving onto Abbey Road: turn left and in a few strides, bear right. The other runs on to emerge on another road: turn right. Both ways soon rejoin, and all that remains is to follow the road out to the beach and the conclusion of the walk.   ●

Crummock Water

		GPS waypoints
Start	Scalehill Bridge	
Distance	8½ miles (13.8km)	
Height gain	1,050 feet (320m)	
Approximate time	4¼ hours	
Parking	Scalehill Bridge (Pay and Display)	
Route terrain	Lakeside rocks and rough ground, occasionally muddy and wet	
Ordnance Survey maps	Landranger 89 (West Cumbria), Explorer OL4 (The English Lakes – North-western area)	

GPS waypoints

- ✏ NY 149 215
- Ⓐ NY 160 199
- Ⓑ NY 168 186
- Ⓒ NY 167 177
- Ⓓ NY 174 169
- Ⓔ NY 150 203

Crummock Water is twice the size of Buttermere lake, and boasts just as beautiful a shoreline. Along with Buttermere and nearby Loweswater, this attractive stretch of water would once have formed one large glacial lake, subsequently split into three by debris washed down from the surrounding high fells. The name of the lake derives from the Celtic, 'cromach', a crook. So, it is the crooked lake, being forced to bend around the stubby knuckle of Hause Point below Rannerdale. Crummock is one of Lakeland's deepest lakes, and was once renowned for its char, a deep-water fish that found its way into such delicacies as potted char and char pie. To walk around Crummock Water is no modest undertaking and likely to be damp in places, but it ranks among the finest valley walks in Lakeland.

✏ To avoid congestion in Buttermere village, the walk starts at the northern end of Crummock Water, although there are other equally suitable starting points on Cinderdale Common or at Hause Point, for example. Leave the Scalehill Bridge car park by following a track into Lanthwaite Wood, briefly following the course of the River Cocker. Pass through a gate and, when the path forks, branch right for about 100 yards and then keep forward to reach the lakeshore.

Walk at the rear of the Boat House, and into an area of newer plantation, crossing stiles a few times before reaching a gate giving into a field. Stay with the lakeshore path to reach Fletcher Field. Stick with the lakeside path to meet a wall and then climb steps to the valley road Ⓐ.

Turn right and head for the car park on Cinderdale Common with the massive bulk of Lad Hows and Grasmoor looming above. Walk up beside Cinderdale Beck for 50 yards and then cross it at a convenient spot. Follow the broad track on the other side, heading towards the shapely outline of Rannerdale Knotts.

The track soon assumes a level course and reaches a gate beyond which it continues into the valley of Rannerdale,

Cinderdale Common and Whiteless Pike

which has now opened up ahead. As the path reaches the entrance to Rannerdale, go down to cross a footbridge spanning Squat Beck **B**.

Rannerdale, for all its undoubted beauty, has something of a sinister history to it, for it was here, at the end of the 11th century, that the people of Buttermere ambushed and slew invading Normans, leaving their bodies to rot at the entrance to the dale. The story is recounted in *The Secret Valley* by Nicolas Size, which relates how 'It was hopeless to try and bury great piles of Norman dead', and how Rannerdale 'was like a charnel house'. Today the spot where the Normans were left is said to burst each spring into an intensely bright carpet of bluebells.

Over Squat Beck, turn right and follow a path below the crags of Rannerdale Knotts to rejoin the valley road. Turn left for a short distance, and then leave the road by branching left onto a rising stony path that crosses above Hause Point before making a gradual descent towards the village of Buttermere, and rejoining the road **C**. Cross the road and go through a gate

leading to the lakeshore. Walk along the lakeshore until you see a gate to your left leading into Nether How woods.

Go through the gate and follow the path through the wood.

The path briefly leads to the lakeshore again before re-entering the wood. Take a path to your left leading through Nether How wood to a footbridge. Cross the bridge and follow the ongoing path to reach the National Trust car park at Buttermere.

Walk out of the car park, and turn right, taking care against approaching traffic, to reach the **Bridge Hotel** and there turn immediately to the right, and onto a track **D** to the left of the **Buttermere Court Hotel**.

The Fish Inn, as the Buttermere Court then was, and the village of Buttermere, was the scene of melodrama in the early 19th century. Accounts of the beauty of 'the Maid of Buttermere', Mary Robinson, daughter of the landlord of the Fish, brought to Buttermere a scoundrel by the name of John Hadfield. He posed as a colonel and member of Parliament, and wooed and

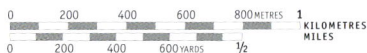

0	200	400	600	800 METRES	1	
						KILOMETRES
						MILES
0	200	400	600 YARDS	½		

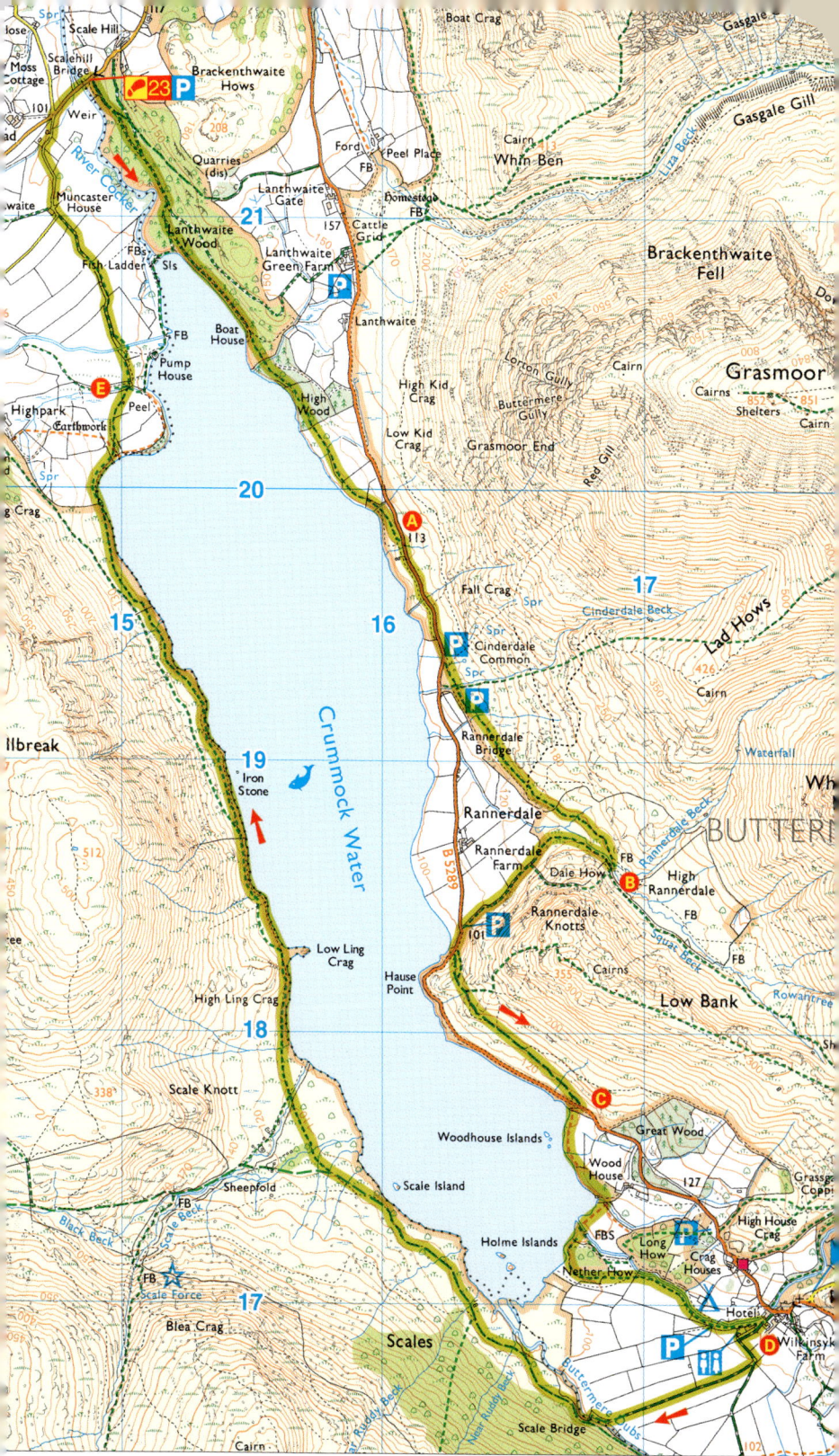

Scale Hill

Moss Cottage

Scalehill Bridge

🅿 23 P

Brackenthwaite Hows

Boat Crag

Gasgale

Gasgale Gill

Weir

River Cocker

101

Muncaster House

waite

Quarries (dis)

Ford

FB

Peel Place

Cairn

Whin Ben

Liza Beck

21

Lanthwaite Gate

Homestead

FB

Brackenthwaite Fell

Fish Ladder

FBs

Sls

Lanthwaite Wood

157

Cattle Grid

160

Lanthwaite Green Farm

Grasmoor

FB

Boat House

Pump House

High Wood

Lanthwaite

High Kid Crag

Lorton Gully

Cairn

852

851

Cairns

Shelters

Cairn

E

Peel

Low Kid Crag

Buttermere Gully

Highpark

Earthwork

20

Grasmoor End

Red Gill

Spr

g Crag

A

113

Fall Crag

Spr

Cinderdale Beck

Lad Hows

15

16

17

P

Cinderdale Common

426

Spr

Ilbreak

Spr

Cairn

P

19

Iron Stone

Crummock Water

Rannerdale Bridge

Waterfall

Rannerdale

Rannerdale Beck

Wh

512

Rannerdale Farm

BUTTER

Squat Beck

Low Ling Crag

B 5289

Dale How

FB

B

High Rannerdale

FB

High Ling Crag

18

P

101

Rannerdale Knotts

Cairns

355

FB

Low Bank

Rowantree

Sh

Hause Point

Scale Knott

338

Woodhouse Islands

C

Great Wood

Grassga Coppi

Sheepfold

FB

Scale Beck

Scale Island

Wood House

127

High House Crag

Black Beck

Holme Islands

FBS

Long How

P

Crag Houses

FB

Scale Force

Nether How

Buttermere Dubs

Hotel

D

Wilkinsyk Farm

17

Blea Crag

Scales

P

Near Ruddy Beck

Scale Bridge

102

Cairn

won Mary, marrying her in Lorton church on the 2 October 1802, just two days before William Wordsworth married Mary Hutchinson. Within days Hadfield was exposed as an impostor, a man already married, a convicted swindler and confidence trickster. He was later caught, tried and hanged, not for bigamy, as might be supposed, but for using his false position as an MP to frank mail, in effect forgery, which in those days carried the death penalty. Numerous accounts have been written about the story, which later found its way onto some London stages, but the most moving is Melvyn Bragg's book *The Maid of Buttermere*. Mary, recovered from her experience and later went on to marry a man from Caldbeck. She lived to a good age, raising seven children, five into adulthood.

Follow a broad track but only as far as a turning on the right (signposted for Scale Force), and take to the ongoing track that leads to Buttermere Dubs, the stream linking Buttermere and Crummock Water, which is crossed by twin-arched Scale Bridge.

Bear right along a path, crossing Near and Far Ruddy Becks and following a line of cairns across a stretch of wet ground to arrive at a large cairn just past a group of three holly trees. Here a path branches left to visit Scale Force, an optional addition to this walk.

Scale Force, a popular attraction with Victorian tourists, at 125 feet (31m) is the highest waterfall in the Lake District, and plummets Scale Beck into a tree-lined cleft from the high combe above. Of course, it is at its best following prolonged rainfall.

The original route may be rejoined either by retracing your steps or by crossing the footbridge below Scale Force and then turning right onto a path that leads across Black Beck. If not visiting Scale Force, simply keep forward, above Crummock Water, on a clear path that leads to Low Ling Crag, a small rocky island sticking out into the lake like a sore thumb.

The next stretch is often wet and slippery as the route crosses numerous streams flowing down from Mellbreak. There are two possible paths, one high, one low. Both lead to a gap in a wall next to the lake. From it, cross two more stiles, and then turn left along a dilapidated wall to the remains of a Peel Tower **E**.

Peel (or Pele) towers date from the late Middle Ages, and were an expression of the uncertainties of existence during the 300 years of the Border Troubles. They are most common in Scotland and Northumberland, and acquired their name because they consisted of a central living tower with a 'peel' or 'pale', that is, a stockade, originally built of earth and logs, but later of stone.

From the tower follow a path north-wards to an access lane at Muncaster House, and take this out to meet the Loweswater road. Turn right to return to the Scalehill Bridge car park. ●

Crummock Water and Mellbreak

Dow Crag and Goat's Water

		GPS waypoints
Start	Torver	🖼️ SD 285 944
Distance	7½ miles (11.9km)	Ⓐ SD 273 964
Height gain	2,395 feet (730m)	Ⓑ SD 258 965
Approximate time	4½ hours	Ⓒ SD 266 983
Parking	Torver village hall car park (with honesty box)	
Route terrain	Rugged mountain tops and tracks; *not advised in poor visibility*	
Ordnance Survey maps	Landranger 96 (Barrow-in-Furness & South Lakeland), Explorer OL6 (The English Lakes – South-western area)	

This is a pleasant but challenging walk making use of old quarry tracks to gain height to the top of Walna Scar, a high mountain pass linking Coniston with Dunnerdale. The way continues along a fine rocky ridge to the top of Dow Crag overlooking Goat's Water, by way of which the walk concludes, although you can quite easily reverse the loop around Goat's Water and the Dow Crag ridge once you reach the Walna Scar Road – there is a good track/path all the way.

The moors above Torver have been settled since prehistoric times. W. G. Collingwood, in *The Lake Counties* writes, 'All these fells must once have been the happy hunting-grounds of primitive races, children of the mist, perhaps surviving long after the outskirts were settled by civilized folk.' Originally a Norse settlement, Torver received its name from the Norse word for turf. A path led through the hamlet from Furness Abbey and was used by the monks. Torver was also a staging post for a packhorse trail over the Walna Scar pass to the Duddon Valley.

Long involved with the many traditional industries of Lakeland – stone and slate quarrying, iron smelting, charcoal production, bobbin manufacture, farming and milling – Torver, overlooking Coniston Water,

developed significantly when the Furness Railway came here in 1859. Farming was also an early enterprise around Torver, and there was a time when the Herdwick sheep far outnumbered people.

Although a 12th-century chapel stood on the site of the present-day church of St Luke, burials were not permitted there until 1538; before then the village's dead had to be carried to Ulverston. When Archbishop Cranmer authorised burials at Torver, the long, bier-laden treks over mountain passes ended. A new church was built in 1849, and that replaced by St Luke's in 1883-4. The nearby Church House Inn as a building dates from the 14th century, but doesn't appear in the records as an inn until 1851, when it is listed as Kirk House Inn.

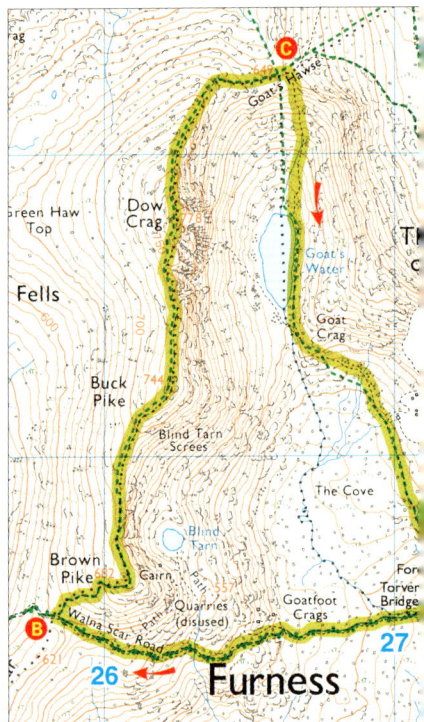

Turn right out of the car park and then, as the road bends right, take the dead-end lane on the left. Ignoring any rougher tracks, keep to the surfaced lane through the hamlet of Scarr Head. It later becomes a walled bridleway. After a gate, keep right as another track branches left. Walk on until you reach a bridge spanning Tranearth Beck, then continue by a rough track to gated sheep pens. Go through the smaller gate on the right to access a bridge over Torver Beck. Once across the bridge turn left to pass along the base of quarry waste heaps, before climbing beside a tree-lined gully – *the entrance to quarry workings, and dangerous.*

Climb to a fence, turn right to circle the edge of the flooded Bannishead Quarry pit and then continue on a broad, grassy cut through the bracken. Bear left at subsequent forks to climb to the Walna Scar Road Ⓐ. Turn left to cross a packhorse bridge over Torver Beck. Once across the bridge the track becomes more eroded as it climbs to a large cairn. Continue, ascending all the while, passing small cairns and a small stone shelter on the right.

A crossing of paths marks the top of the Walna Scar Road, a high mountain

Dow Crag and Buck Pike from Walna Scar

pass Ⓑ from where there is a fine view down into Dunnerdale. Turn right and ascend a constructed path to a stone shelter on the top of Brown Pike, the first of two fell tops en route to Dow Crag. From here on, the views are consistently impressive, and the high-level walking of supreme quality.

From the shelter the path heads north along the rim of the corrie that houses

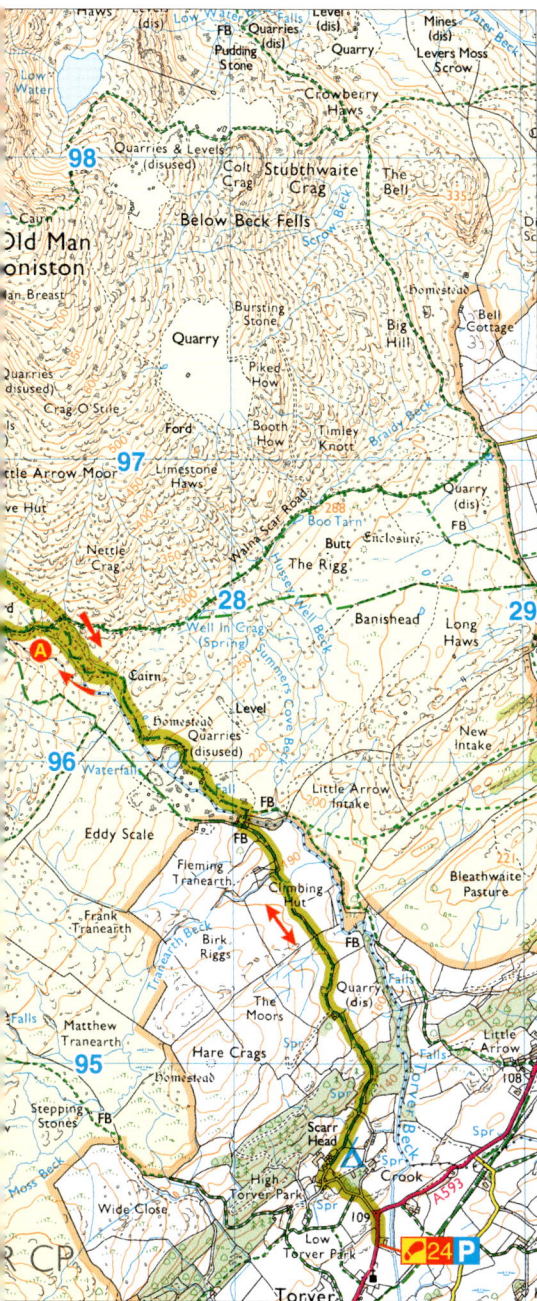

Dow Crag by a stony path. As you approach Dow Crag, the immense cliffs falling to Goat's Water below become more pronounced and the path crosses the top of one or two yawning gullies; *children will need close supervision here, and while on the fine rocky summit of Dow Crag.*

From this point everything is downhill, but only physically. You may be leaving behind the magnificent views from the top of Dow Crag, but the return beside Goat's Water is walking of the highest order.

From the top of Dow Crag go north, continuing your original direction, on a clear rocky path which soon turns north-east to descend to Goat's Hawse 🅲, a boggy col linking Dow Crag and the Old Man of Coniston.

Go down to the Hawse and as the path starts to ascend on the other side take a path off to the right and descend to Goat's Water on a good, stone-pitched path.

Use the path along the eastern shore of Goat's Water, passing through scattered boulders, and out of this side valley, to a cairn on the Walna Scar Road, not far from the point at which you first joined it.

Cross the track to a green path, swinging right in a further 350 yards to regain your outward route and retrace your steps to Torver. ●

Blind Tarn. Press on along the ridge, crossing another minor summit, Buck Pike, on the way, and then heading for

Place Fell

Start	Patterdale
Distance	7 miles (11.5km)
Height gain	2,265 feet (690m)
Approximate time	4½ hours
Parking	Opposite Patterdale Hotel (Pay and Display)
Route terrain	Rough fell walking; stony tracks; steep ascent and descent
Ordnance Survey maps	Landranger 90 (Penrith & Keswick), Explorer OL5 (The English Lakes – North-eastern area)

GPS waypoints

- NY 396 159
- Ⓐ NY 408 158
- Ⓑ NY 414 179
- Ⓒ NY 417 192
- Ⓓ NY 398 162

Place Fell perches above Ullswater rather like a broody hen; the only significant fell to closely flank Patterdale. The main upthrust of summits to the west lean back from the dale, while north-east from Place Fell the fells diminish in size, although they are no less appealing. Throw in a rather spectacular shoreline on the east side of the lake along which to return, and an ascent of Place Fell suddenly rockets in popularity.

There is a convenient parking area opposite the **Patterdale Hotel**, and from this turn left along the road (it's safer if you cross it), and go past the odd-shaped **White Lion** (**toilets**, if needed, soon appear on the right).

'Patterdale' is the name given both to the valley and its principal community, described in Baddeley's *Guide to the English Lake District* as 'one of the most

Place Fell and Ullswater

charmingly situated in Britain, and in itself clean and comely.' Many villages, like Patterdale, were often presided over by one dominant family. In Patterdale it was the Mounseys, called the 'Kings of Patterdale', who lived at Patterdale Hall at the entrance to Grisedale.

The dale is especially pleasant, and is probably named after St Patrick, one of three eminent missionaries (along with St Ninian and St Kentigern) thought to have trawled this area on evangelical missions during the early years of the 5th century. Although there is a 'through-route' along Patterdale, it somehow retains a quiet aloofness, certainly when compared with the bustle of Ambleside and Windermere beyond the protective sleeping policeman of the Kirkstone Pass. Stay on the main road, but shortly take the first turning on the left, a narrow

lane that crosses Goldrill Beck, and leads to the hamlet of Rooking. Walk past the houses to a gate on the right giving on to a path for 'Boredale Hause and Angle Tarn'.

A fine path, pitched in places, now slants in a south-easterly direction across the base of Place Fell. The views just seem to get better the more you ascend, and provide a welcome distraction from the effort, such as it is. To the south west there are particularly fine glimpses into Deepdale and Dovedale, while to the south the road slips past Brotherswater and climbs the Kirkstone Pass.

When the ascending path forks, keep

left and gradually work a way up to the broad col known as Boredale Hause **A**. Boredale is actually the next dale, running in a north-easterly direction, sandwiched between Place Fell and Beda Fell. Mark Richards, a latter-day doyen of Lakeland fell wandering explains that both Wordsworth and Wainwright made the mistake of assuming Boredale Hause had something to do with pigs, and hence used the spelling Boardale. In the ancient languages of Britain, the Scandinavian for pig was 'grise', and the Celtic-British was 'moch'. Boredale, he suggests, simply means 'the valley with a storehouse'.

In the hause you will find some stone ruins, said to be those of a chapel, but looking remarkably like a collapsed sheepfold. It would have been incredibly small, and some, including Dorothy Wordsworth, cast doubt on whether it was really a place of worship or simply a shelter, but a chapel here would have been logical given that the route was a busy crossing point between Patterdale and Martindale. It was Captain Luff of nearby Side Farm who showed the chapel to the Wordsworths, describing it as a place where the inhabitants of Martindale and Patterdale were accustomed to meet on Sabbath days. The chapel featured in Wordsworth's poem *The Excursion*, the story of a 'poor old man' overtaken by a storm while climbing onto the fell to collect peat, who used the chapel as a shelter.

At Boredale Hause you abandon the main trail, the Coast-to-Coast, which now wanders off in a southerly direction. Instead turn northwards and take to a clear, grassy path that ambles up onto the south ridge of Place Fell.

There is no doubt about the route. But console yourself with frequent stops to take in the spectacular scenery all around, and soon you find yourself at the trig pillar on the summit, flanked by a number of nooks and crannies in which to take a break. Another, nearby point holds a cairn, competing, probably vainly for the distinction of being the highest point.

The onward route lies in a north-easterly direction, passing a large pool and descending grassy slopes to a small depression at Low Moss **B**. On passing a ruined sheepfold take a path on the left that strikes down a shallow valley targeting an area of slate spoil. A grassy path continues. When it forks, keep left, heading into the clutches of Scalehow Beck. Scalehow Force is not natural. What is now the Ullswater Outward Bound School was once a private mansion, the owner of which blasted the beck to create a waterfall in an effort to improve his view. Surprising in a way because the forward view of Sandwick Bay is really quite special.

The path leads down to a junction with another path, a bridleway **C**, and here turn left, crossing Scalehow Beck by a footbridge and rejoicing in one of the finest and most popular paths in Lakeland. What makes it so popular is the steamer service on the lake, which brings walkers across to Howtown from where they can walk back behind Hallin Fell.

Flanking the north-west foot slopes of Place Fell, the path now heads for Silver Bay, and then speeds off southwards across Blowick meadows to reach Side Farm **D**. Here turn right, between the farm buildings, and take a fine, broad track out to the valley road, re-crossing Goldrill Beck en route. When you reach the road, you may feel like diverting to the right to visit St Patrick's Church. But otherwise, turn left, and soon find yourself at the entrance to the car park.　●

The Coledale Horseshoe

		GPS waypoints	
Start	Stoneycroft		NY 232 217
Distance	9 miles (14.5km)	**A**	NY 204 205
Height gain	3,885 feet (1,185m)	**B**	NY 189 212
Approximate time	6 hours	**C**	NY 230 236
Parking	Roadside at Stoneycroft		
Route terrain	Mainly high fell paths, some craggy sections		
Ordnance Survey maps	Landranger 90 (Penrith & Keswick), Explorer OL4 (The English Lakes – North-western area)		

This fine circuit of Coledale is a magnificent outing and a test of fitness; it is a good, healthy day's exercise, and one best left for a fine day, although winter walkers will enjoy the circuit, suitably equipped, of course. The circuit begins by heading for the knobbly summit of Causey Pike, a distinctive picture-postcard backdrop to the town of Keswick. The complete circuit is quite demanding, although there are two useful cut out points should they be needed.

There is usually room to park cars along the road into Newlands, including a sizeable pull-off just west of Uzzicar. From here walk south along the road to Stoneycroft Bridge, just beyond which, at a very low signpost, a footpath branches right up steps and very quickly gets to grips with a path that ascends steadily across the northern slopes of Rowling End; indeed, strong walkers can deviate and include Rowling End in the round.

The slanting path rises to a col linking Rowling End with Causey Pike. The final pull to the summit is rocky and quite delightful, and the fact that it may require the use of hands near the top need deter no one.

Once the summit of Causey Pike is underfoot, the long ridge to Crag Hill comes fully into view, rippling away into the distance, with fine views in virtually all directions. Immediately to the north, sitting in the bowl formed by Coledale, are Outside and Barrow, while the final summit of the circuit, Grisedale Pike rises in the distance.

Continue south of west along the

Hobcarton Crags

ridge following a good path to gain Scar Crags, the next summit and a little higher than Causey Pike. Cross a small grassy plateau before descending to the col with Sail, which, end-on, looks far more daunting than it is. The col **Ⓐ** is the first available escape route back to the start should it be needed, heading down along a track originally engineered to service a cobalt mine farther up the valley. Lower down it passes south of Outside and before

reaching Stile End, bears right to follow Stoneycroft Gill.

Onward and upward the ascent of Sail is unremarkable; not so the final section of this ridge up to Crag Hill, which is exhilarating if sadly far too short. This is a narrow link with the higher fell, and concludes up a narrow crest to the summit, the highest point of this circuit.

A direct descent from Crag Hill to Coledale Hause should not be considered; the ground is broken and loose, steep and unstable. The safer option lies in heading west from the top of Crag Hill,

as if heading for Grasmoor, and then at the col between the two mountains, turning right (north) along the right bank of Gasgale Gill to reach the broad expanse that is Coledale Hause **B**.

Here lies the second escape route, taking a prominent and cairned path, passing Force Crag into Coledale Valley and following this all the way down to Braithwaite.

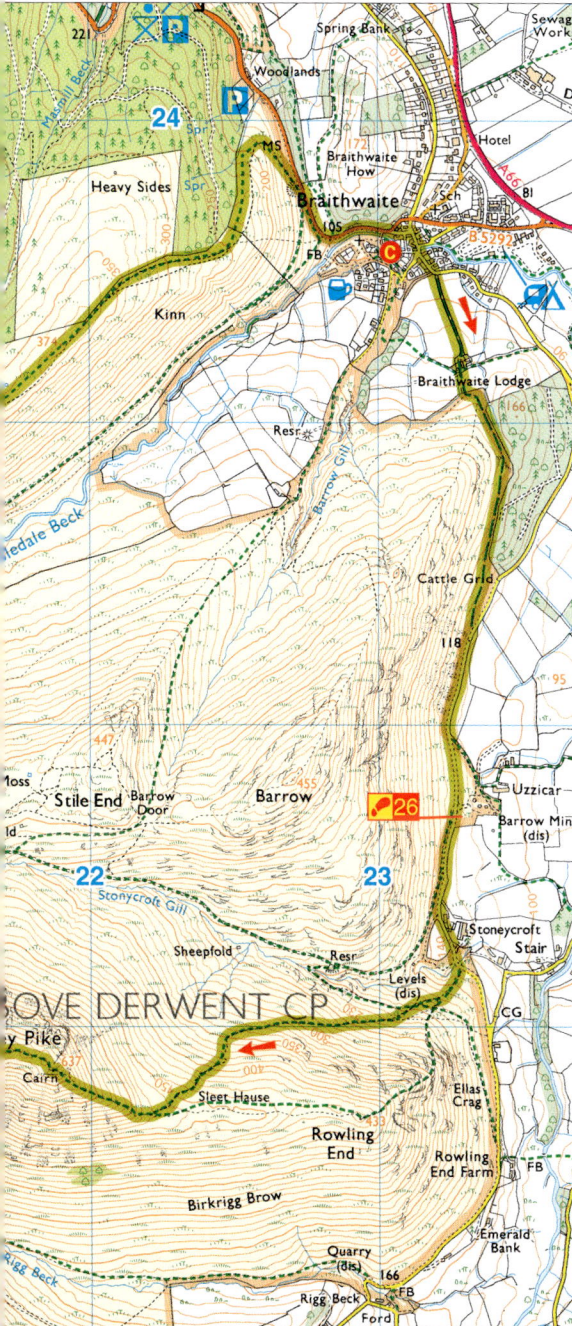

The continuation to Grisedale Pike from Coledale Hause is obvious enough, slanting upwards in a north-easterly direction to pass first over a minor top before continuing to Grisedale Pike itself.

The descent from Grisedale Pike has always been rather loose and awkward, but a clear path romps steeply down to Sleet How, and then by stages along the ridge south of Hospital Plantation to emerge on the Whinlatter road just above Braithwaite.

Now walk down into Braithwaite, and investigate the narrow lanes to locate the road for Newlands **C**. Set off along this, but very soon leave it at the turning for Braithwaite Lodge. Walk up past the farm, as if heading onto Barrow, but once on the base of the fell, bear left to follow a clear route alongside a small plantation beyond which you emerge onto the Newlands road, along which a short walk completes the route. ●

Wet Sleddale, Swindale and Mosedale

		GPS waypoints	
Start	Wet Sleddale	✏	NY 555 114
Distance	12½ miles (17.5km)	Ⓐ	NY 559 128
Height gain	1,540 feet (470m)	Ⓑ	NY 537 144
Approximate time	6 hours	Ⓒ	NY 514 132
Parking	Wet Sleddale Reservoir	Ⓓ	NY 506 100
Route terrain	Extreme moorland; hard surface tracks; minor road walking	Ⓔ	NY 534 112
Ordnance Survey maps	Landranger 90 (Penrith & Keswick), Explorer OL5 (The English Lakes – North-eastern area)		

This long walk into a remote valley generates heaps of rugged and enjoyable moorland tramping around the ancient Ralfland Forest. Hard-surfaced service roads speed progress across some sections, while the shapely landscapes of Swindale and Mosedale expose the walker to the rarely visited folds of eastern Lakeland. This is a walk to be savoured leisurely, preferably on a good, clear day.

Although there is an ideal parking area at the south-eastern edge of Wet Sleddale Reservoir, if this is full, you can park, off-road and considerably, at Cooper's Green (NY 558 122), close by the footbridge spanning the embryonic River Lowther. In any case, you have to walk the road between the two points.

✏ Beyond the footbridge a gate gives access through a wall and onto a narrow lane. Turn right and follow the lane for 440 yards, until you rejoin the river, and then go left to follow a riverside path. Another 440 yards brings you to a service road Ⓐ that crosses the moors to Mardale. Turn left along this, striding freely and quickly with views of the hamlet of Keld and then of Shap Abbey. When you intercept the lane from Keld, go left bound for Tailbert Farm.

Just as you reach the first enclosed pasture of Tailbert, leave the road for an initially stony track Ⓑ cutting across the hillside. The track soon deteriorates into a less distinct grassy trod, leading on across the gorse and bracken flanks of Dog Hill, where Swindale eases into view below. The valley curves progressively southwards to an abrupt end, where a corpse road from Mardale enters the valley en route for Shap.

When you reach the valley bottom, there is a choice of a ford and stepping stones or a nearby bridge Ⓒ; both put you on the valley road. Turn left and walk to Swindale Head.

Go through a series of gates at Swindale Head and onto a bridleway for Mosedale, heading into the end of the dale where the fellsides rise steeply to Selside Pike and Swindale Common.

Wet Sleddale

Above the dale head, Mosedale Beck flows through a shallow, V-shaped moorland valley before plummeting into Swindale Forces. Nearby Hobgrumble Gill fills a dark gash in the cliff face, formed by waters seeping from a high corrie on Selside Pike. The streams combine amid glacial moraine to produce Swindale Beck, a bright treat in a sombre craggy dale.

Mosedale and Hobgrumble corrie are both hanging valleys, fashioned by the weight of ice that ground away at the sediments and rocks of the main valley floor. This whole region is populated by red deer that roam freely across the moors; pass this way in autumn and you will hear the bellowing of stags at the rut. Other than on foot or horseback there is no way through Swindale. The sense of remoteness is supreme.

Here, after the Romans had returned to sunnier climes, the Vikings came. Old maps show the name 'Thengeheved' below Gouther Crag on the south side of the dale. This was an ancient meeting place of Viking chiefs who would gather beneath the crag to settle the affairs of their communities. There is another in Little Langdale, but even more are surely lost to posterity. Now those same cliffs shelter peregrine, buzzard and winter flocks of travel-weary fieldfare, mistle thrush, redwing and brambling.

The valley was bought from the Lowther Estate by the then National Water Board who drew up plans to flood the dale; thankfully the outbreak of the Second World War put a stop to the plans, but not before the chapel and school at Truss Gap were demolished.

A walled track leads to a final building on the left, just beyond which it forks. Branch left. Beyond a final gate the ongoing track winds through moraine giving onto a grassy path that continues to take the route into Mosedale, winding upwards through the rocky outcrops of Selside Pike. The higher the path goes, the less distinct does it seem as it continues across open moorland to meet a fence at Swine Gill. Pass through a gate and press on to a nearby dilapidated building and a collapsed wall.

Follow the wall until a footbridge comes into view down on the left spanning Mosedale Beck. Stay on the path until you encounter a vehicle track cutting down to the bridge, known locally as Bog Bridge **D**, and with good reason. On the other side, more tracks climb onto a broad ridge, rising to meet a fence and gate. Beyond this, a conspicuous grassy track climbs farther. When this forks, branch right. To the south-west, the distant Mosedale Cottage, surrounded by a stand of trees, lies midway between Swindale and Longsleddale, and is a forlorn spot below the spoil of the disused Mosedale Quarry.

Leaving this empty quarter, the walk climbs into Wet Sleddale, before beginning a long, easy descent just as the reservoir comes into view. After a second stile **E**, just north-west of

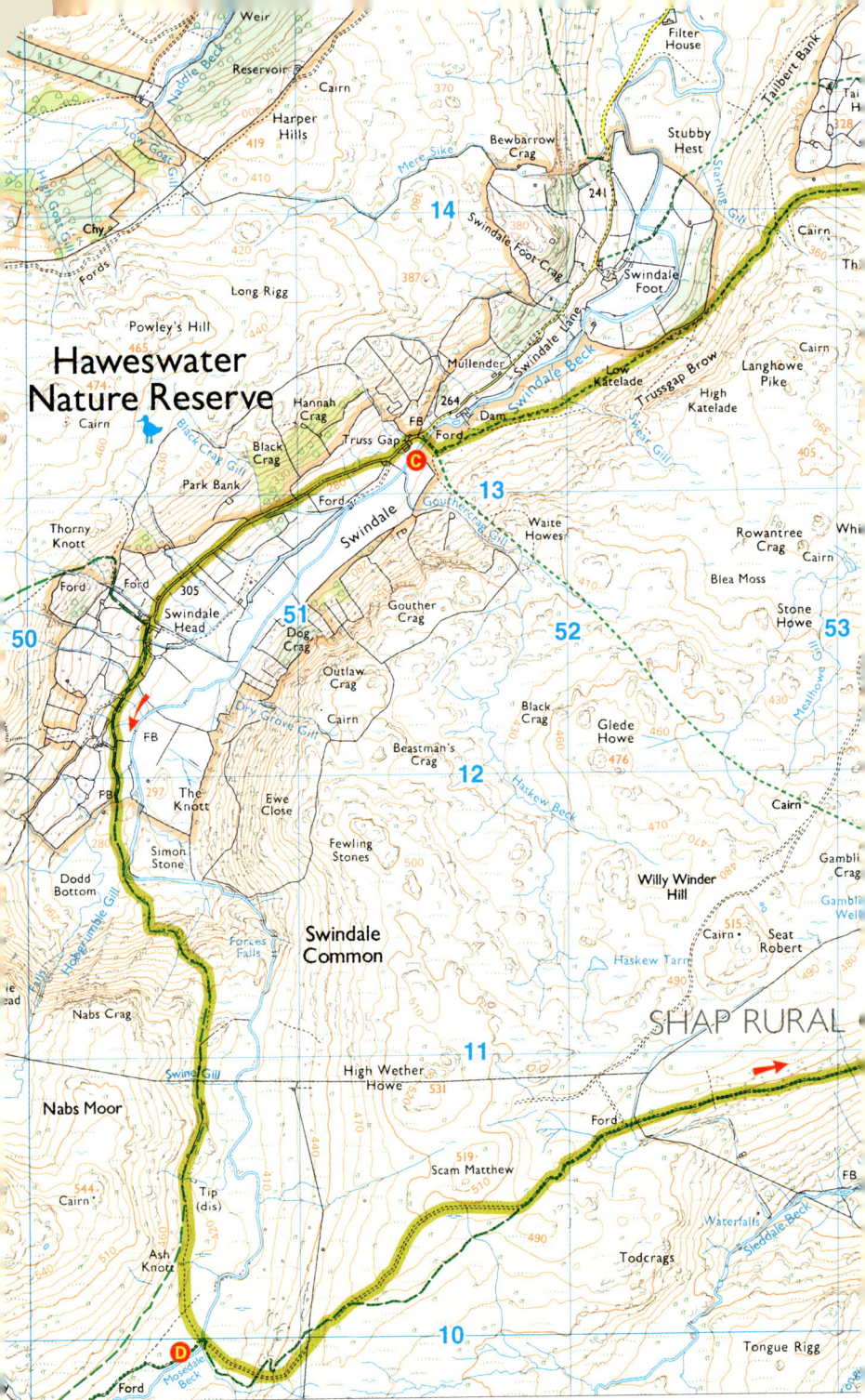

Sleddale Hall, turn right down zigzags that take you to the isolated farmstead at Sleddale Hall.

Sleddale Hall was the unlikely setting for the 1986 cult film classic *Withnail and I*, starring Richard E. Grant in his

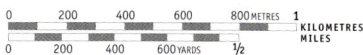

first film role, and Paul McGann, who made his name in the BBC serial *The Monocled Mutineer,* and for briefly portraying the eighth 'Doctor Who' in the television movie.

Withnail and I, features two 'resting' actors, fed up with damp, cold piles of washing-up, mad drug dealers and psychotic Irishmen, they decide to leave their squalid Camden flat for an idyllic holiday in the countryside. But when they get there it rains non-stop, there's no food, and their basic survival skills are virtually non-existent. Wet Sleddale was perfectly type cast, and Sleddale Hall, which dates from the 18th century, became Crow Cragg in the film. Descend from Sleddale Hall to cross Sleddale Beck and then follow a clear track along the south side of the reservoir back to the parking area.

The Four Passes

		GPS waypoints
Start	Wasdale Head	🖋 NY 187 085
Distance	15 miles (24km); 13½ miles (21.6km) via Haystacks	Ⓐ NY 192 114
Height gain	(full circuit) 4,430 feet (1,350m); (via Haystacks) 3,625 feet (1,105m)	Ⓑ NY 189 133
		Ⓒ NY 225 136
Approximate time	(full circuit) 9 hours; (via Haystacks) 8 hours	Ⓓ NY 235 122
		Ⓔ NY 235 109
Parking	Wasdale	Ⓕ NY 222 099
Route terrain	Rugged mountain tracks; some road walking	
Ordnance Survey maps	Landranger 90 (Penrith and Keswick), Explorers OL4 (The English Lakes – North-western area) and OL6 (The English Lakes – South-western area)	

Suitable even for days when the tops are draped in mist, the Four Passes walk is an utterly refreshing circuit that slips neatly into any serious walker's portfolio; it is, however, a significant undertaking, suitable only for strong walkers. Its basic construction is simple: you link the valleys of Wasdale, Ennerdale, Buttermere and Borrowdale by crossing four passes: Black Sails, Scarth Gap, Honister and Sty Head. Being circular, and touching base in each valley, you can plug into the circuit anywhere.

Mosedale awaits, and at its head, the great bulk of Pillar, an inevitable attraction for anyone based in Wasdale and Ennerdale. Both these valleys have long been popular with walkers, though their relative inaccessibility tends to keep out the idly curious.

🖋 At Wasdale Head, go past the inn and onto the track that leads into Mosedale, trekking round the base of Kirk Fell, before rising a little more sternly by Gatherstone Beck to Black Sail Pass Ⓐ. From this mountain pass there is an undulating trod crossing from just below Black Sail Pass to Beck Head, between Great Gable and Kirk Fell (East top), and from there following Moses' Trod to Honister. Moses is said to have been an illicit whisky distiller,

working furtively on the slopes of Fleetwith Pike; more likely he was helping himself to plumbago, which in those days brought a good price, especially on the black market.

Onward the route descends sharply to the head of Ennerdale, arriving without complication at Black Sail Youth Hostel, one of the most imaginatively sited youth hostels in England, and an ideal base for anyone wanting to tackle this walk or the ascent of surrounding peaks over a few days.

Traffic is prohibited in Ennerdale, and results in the preservation here of a wild and rugged landscape. The once serried ranks of conifer that flanked the valley have seen some realignment, felling and replanting in recent years that has eased much of Ennerdale Forest's former rigidity, making it an altogether better place to wander.

Beyond the youth hostel, the walk keeps to the northern edge of the forest, rising easily to Scarth Gap **B**, with the great scree slope of Gamlin End rising to High Crag on the one hand, and less demanding Haystacks on the other. From here a path descending to Gatesgarth Farm at the head of the Buttermere Valley is pursued, there heading east, up the B5289 for the top of Honister **C**. Such, at least, is the conventional route, but walking up a road pass is unlikely to appeal to many when a vastly superior alternative is to hand.

*(From Scarth Gap a variant route – linking **B** and **C** – heads up the rock shoulder of Haystacks, and from there out across the great plateau of knolls and hollows between Haystacks and Honister. Innominate Tarn is first reached, a place of some poignancy for walkers reared on the Lakeland gospels according to the late Alfred Wainwright. Blackbeck Tarn, a little farther on has rather less appeal, though Nature's architecture here perfectly frames a picture of Buttermere beyond Warnscale Bottom. On crossing Black Beck a path ascends to the remains of Dubs Quarry, where a few ruinous buildings mark the start of a long gradual climb to a point overlooking the slate quarry at Honister.)*

A short way down the road from Honister Hause a track branches left. This was the original line down to Borrowdale, and a toll road that now sees a steady flow of pedestrian traffic. As Seatoller is reached, the old road swings round to meet the new road at a gate.

Now walk down to the branching road from Seatoller to Seathwaite Farm **D**. Beyond the farm buildings, a broad path escorts the combined forces of Styhead Gill and Grains Gill, here the River Derwent, as far as the old packhorse bridge, Stockley Bridge **E**. Through a gate, ignoring a track going left beside a wall, a path ahead injects a little ascent, pulling up towards a small plantation that conceals the white mare's tail of Taylorgill Force. Climbing steadily, a rough track presses on to a wooden bridge spanning Styhead Gill, beyond which Styhead Tarn **F** reposes in a vast hollow flanked by some of the highest of Lakeland's mountains – Great Gable, Lingmell, Scafell Pike, Broad Crag, Great End.

(Between Seathwaite and the wooden bridge spanning Styhead Gill, a variant route, with a better view of Taylorgill Force, is available. This leaves Seathwaite by an archway through barns, as if heading for Sour Milk Gill and the hanging valley of Gillercombe. Once the Derwent, is crossed, however, a path, initially muddy, skirts the bottom of a small copse, roughly parallel with the Stockley Bridge path. Gradually, this climbs and later turns the corner of Base Brown and scampers to a gate in a most curious spot. A little nimble footwork on easy rising rocks soon leads on towards Taylorgill Force, followed by a steady rise, keeping close by Styhead Gill, to the wooden bridge and, before long, Sty Head Pass.)

Sty Head is unquestionably one of the finest spots in Lakeland, and a popular crossroads as walkers launch themselves in all directions. Not surprisingly a number of tracks radiate from Sty Head, and a little caution is needed to get the right one, heading down towards Wasdale, high above Lingmell Beck.

The valley bottom is reached near Burnthwaite Farm, one of only a few farms remaining active in Wasdale. From here it is just a short way to complete the walk.

Close

Waterfalls

B 5289

Gatesgarth Farm

15

Gatesgarthdale Beck

Peggy's Bridge (FB)

Gatesgarth Cottage

Weir

Meml

156

Moss Crag

Low Crag

Fords

High Raven Crag

Low Raven Crag

High Crag Butresse

Buttermere Fell

Warnscale

Warnscale Bottom

Fleetwith Edge

Honister Crag

Burnt Scarth

Black Crag

phone utresse

High Wax Knott

Low Wax Knott

14

Ford

Fleetwith Pike

White Cove

High Crag

744

Striddle Crag

Honister Qua (dis)

Quarry (dis)

Gamlin End

Marble Stone

FB

Cairn

Scarth Gap

Level (dis)

Fords

Dubs Quarry (disused)

Disma

Seat

561

BPs

B

Scarth Gap

Cairn

Path

Little Round How

Sheepfold

Hay Stacks

Quarry (dis)

Dubs Bottom

Cairn

Green Crag

13

Great Round How

Innominate Tarn

Dub's Quarry (dis)

Blackbeck Tarn

Waterfall

Raven Crag

inson's airn

River Liza

Ford

Black Sail Hut

BPs

12

Seavy Knott

BPs

Brandreth

Gove

Proud Knott

Ashcrag Holme

FB

Ash Crag

Cairn

Bnn Crag

Mosey Trod

Looking Stead

Cloven Stone

Pile of Stones

19

20

21

Tongue

Tongue Bck

18

Murt Rigg

A

Kirkfell Crags

Boat How

11

Greengable Crag

Stone Cove

BP

Gatherstone Beck

Black Sail Pass

Pile of Stones

Boat How Crags

Baysoar Slack

Beckhead Tarn

Gable Crag

Great Gable

Gatherstone Head

Sheepfold

Pile of Stones

Pile of Stones

Cairn Shelter Cairn

Kirkfell Tarn

Rib End

Beck Head

Meml

Cairn

Westmorland Cairn

Mosedale

Sheepfold

Mosedale Crags

Kirk Fell

Pile of Stones

Well Head

White Napes

Sheepfold

Highnose Head

Holmgill Knotts

Great Napes

Napes Needle

Raven Crag

Mosedale Beck

lder

rghead crees

Gavel Neese

Lower Kern Knotts

Waterfall

Birker Holes

Wasdale Fell

Falls

Sheepfold

Bursting Knott

Waterfall

Ritson's Force (Waterfall)

Mosey Trod (Path)

Ford

Fall

Lingmell Beck

Sheepfold

09

Fog Mire

Burnthwaite

FB

10

Wasdale Head

Row Head

Hotel

28

P

Hutching's How

Lingmell Crag

Down in the Dale

SCALE 1:31250 or 2 INCHES to 1 MILE 3.2CM to 1KM

Further Information

Safety on the Hills

The hills, mountains and moorlands of Britain, though of modest height compared with those in many other countries, need to be treated with respect. Friendly and inviting in good weather, they can quickly be transformed into wet, misty, windswept and potentially dangerous areas of wilderness in bad weather. Even on an outwardly fine and settled summer day, conditions can rapidly deteriorate at high altitudes and, in winter, even more so.

Therefore it is advisable to always take both warm and waterproof clothing, sufficient nourishing food, a hot drink, first-aid kit, torch and whistle. Wear suitable footwear, such as strong walking-boots or shoes that give a good grip over rocky terrain and on slippery slopes. Try to obtain a local weather forecast and bear it in mind before you start. Do not be afraid to abandon your proposed route and return to your starting point in the event of a sudden and unexpected deterioration in the weather. Do not go alone and allow enough time to finish the walk well before nightfall.

Most of the walks described in this book do not venture into remote wilderness areas and will be safe to do, given due care and respect, at any time of year in all but the most unreasonable weather. Indeed, a crisp, fine winter day often provides perfect walking conditions, with firm ground underfoot and a clarity that is not possible to achieve in the other seasons of the year. A few walks, however, are suitable only for reasonably fit and experienced hill walkers able to use a compass and should definitely not be tackled by anyone else during the winter months or in bad weather, especially high winds and mist. These are indicated in the general description that precedes each of the walks.

Walkers and the Law

The Countryside and Rights of Way Act (CRoW Act 2000) gives a public right of access in England and Wales to land mapped as open country (mountain, moor, heath and down) or registered common land. These areas are known as *open access land*, and include land around the coastline, known as *coastal margin*.

Where You Can Go
Rights of Way
Prior to the introduction of the CRoW Act, walkers could only legally access the countryside along public rights of way. These are either 'footpaths' (for walkers only) or 'bridleways' (for walkers, riders on horse-back and pedal cyclists). A third category called 'Byways open to all traffic' (BOATs), is used by motorised vehicles as well as those using non-mechanised transport. Mainly they are green lanes, farm and estate roads, although occasionally they will be found crossing mountainous area.

Rights of way are marked on Ordnance Survey maps. Look for the green broken lines on the Explorer maps, or the red dashed lines on Landranger maps.

The term 'right of way' means exactly what it says. It gives a right of passage over what, for the most part, is private land. Under pre-CRoW legislation walkers were required to keep to the line of the right of way and not stray onto land on either side. If you did inadvertently wander off the right of way, either because of faulty map reading or because the route was not clearly indicated on the ground, you were technically trespassing.

Local authorities have a legal obligation to ensure that rights of way are kept clear and free of obstruction, and are signposted where they leave metalled roads. The duty of local authorities to install signposts extends to the placing of signs along a path or way, but only where the authority considers it necessary to have a signpost or waymark to assist persons unfamiliar with the locality.

CRoW Access Rights
Access Land
As well as being able to walk on existing rights of way, under CRoW legislation you have access to large areas of open land and, under further legislation, a right of coastal access, which is being implemented by Natural England, giving for the first time the right of access around all England's open coast. This includes plans for an England Coast Path (ECP) which will run for 2,795 miles (4,500 kilometres). A corresponding Wales Coast Path has been open since 2012.

Coastal access rights apply within the coastal margin (including along the ECP) unless the land falls into a category of excepted land or is subject to local restrictions, exclusions or diversions.

You can of course continue to use rights of way to cross access land, but you can lawfully leave the path and wander at will in these designated areas.

Where to Walk
Access Land is shown on Ordnance Survey maps by a light yellow tint surrounded by a pale orange border. New orange coloured 'i' symbols on the maps will show the location of permanent access information boards installed by the access authorities. Coastal Margin is shown on Ordnance Survey Explorer maps by a pink tint.

Restrictions
The right to walk on access land may lawfully be restricted by landowners. Landowners can, for any reason, restrict access for up to 28 days in any year. They cannot however close the land:
• on bank holidays;
• for more than four Saturdays and Sundays in a year;
• on any Saturday from 1 June to 11 August; or
• on any Sunday from 1 June to the end of September.
They have to provide local authorities

with five working days' notice before the date of closure unless the land involved is an area of less than five hectares or the closure is for less than four hours. In these cases land-owners only need to provide two hours' notice.

Whatever restrictions are put into place on access land they have no effect on existing rights of way, and you can continue to walk on them.

Dogs
Dogs can be taken on access land, but must be kept on leads of two metres or less between 1 March and 31 July, and at all times where they are near livestock. In addition landowners may impose a ban on all dogs from fields where lambing takes place for up to six weeks in any year. Dogs may be banned from moorland used for grouse shooting and breeding for up to five years.

In the main, walkers following the routes in this book will continue to follow existing rights of way, but a knowledge and understanding of the law as it affects walkers, plus the ability to distinguish access land marked on the maps, will enable anyone who wishes to depart from paths that cross access land either to take a shortcut, to enjoy a view or to explore.

General Obstructions
Obstructions can sometimes cause a problem on a walk and the most common of these is where the path across a field has been ploughed over. It is legal for a farmer to plough up a path provided that it is restored within two weeks. This does not always happen and you are faced with the dilemma of following the line of the path, even if this means treading on crops, or walking round the edge of the field. Although the later course of action seems the most sensible, it does mean that you would be trespassing.

Other obstructions can vary from overhanging vegetation to wire fences across the path, locked gates or even a cattle feeder on the path.

Use common sense. If you can get round the obstruction without causing damage, do

Further Information

so. Otherwise only remove as much of the obstruction as is necessary to secure passage.

If the right of way is blocked and cannot be followed, there is a long-standing view that in such circumstances there is a right to deviate, but this cannot wholly be relied on. Although it is accepted in law that highways (and that includes rights of way) are for the public service, and if the usual track is impassable, it is for the general good that people should be entitled to pass into another line. However, this should not be taken as indicating a right to deviate whenever a way becomes impassable. If in doubt, retreat.

Report obstructions to the local authority and/or the Ramblers.

Useful Organisations

Campaign for National Parks
Tel. 020 3096 7714
cnp.org.uk

Campaign to Protect Rural England (CPRE)
Tel. 020 7981 2800
cpre.org.uk

Forestry England
North England Area office
Tel. 0300 067 4200
forestryengland.uk

Friends of the Lake District
Tel. 01539 720788
friendsofthelakedistrict.org.uk

Lake District National Park Visitor Centre
Tel. 015394 46601
lakedistrict.gov.uk

National Trust
nationaltrust.org.uk

Natural England
Tel. 0300 060 3900
gov.uk/government/organisations/
natural-england

Ordnance Survey
ordnancesurvey.co.uk

Ramblers
Tel. 020 3961 3300
ramblers.org.uk

Tourist Information Centres
Bowness-on-Windermere: 0845 901 0845
Brockhole on Windermere: 015394 46601
Broughton-in-Furness: 01229 716115
Cockermouth: 01900 822634
Coniston: 015394 41533
Egremont: 01946 820693
Glenridding/Ullswater: 0845 901 0845
Keswick: 01539 724555
Penrith: 01768 867466
Whinlatter Visitor Centre: 017687 78469
Windermere: 015394 46499

Youth Hostels Association
Tel. 01629 592600 or 0800 019 1700
yha.org.uk

Ordnance Survey maps for the Lake District

The Lake District is covered by Ordnance Survey 1:50 000 (1¼ inches to 1 mile or 2cm to 1km) scale Landranger map sheets 85, 86, 89, 90, 91, 96, 97 and 98. These all-purpose maps are packed with information to help you explore the area. Viewpoints, picnic sites, places of interest and caravan and camping sites are shown, as well as public rights of way information such as footpaths and bridleways.

To examine the Lake District in more detail, and especially if you are planning walks, Ordnance Survey Explorer maps at 1:25 000 (2½ inches to 1 mile or 4cm to 1km) scale are ideal. Four such maps cover the main Lake District National Park:

OL4 (The English Lakes – North-western area)
OL5 (The English Lakes – North-eastern area)
OL6 (The English Lakes – South-western area)
OL7 (The English Lakes – South-eastern area)

Text:	Terry Marsh; updated text for the 2025 edition, Vivienne Crow
Photography:	Terry Marsh; page 62, © Rob Duncalf/Shutterstock.
	Front cover: © Shaun Barr/Shutterstock
Editorial:	Ark Creative (UK) Ltd
Design:	Ark Creative (UK) Ltd

ISBN 978-0-319-09207-1

While every care has been taken to ensure the accuracy of the route directions, the
publishers cannot accept responsibility for errors or omissions, or for changes in details
given. The countryside is not static: hedges and fences can be removed, stiles can be
replaced by gates, field boundaries can be altered, footpaths can be rerouted and changes
in ownership can result in the closure or diversion of some concessionary paths. Also,
paths that are easy and pleasant for walking in fine conditions may become slippery,
muddy and difficult in wet weather, while stepping stones across rivers and streams may
become impassable.

 If you find an inaccuracy in either the text or maps, please contact Milestone
Publishing at the address below.

First published 2011 by Crimson Publishing.

First published 2021 by Trotman Publishing.

This edition first published 2025 by Milestone Publishing.

Milestone Publishing, 18E Charles Street, Bath, BA1 1HX
pathfinderwalks.co.uk

Printed in India by Replika Press Pvt. Ltd. 3/25

MIX
Paper | Supporting
responsible forestry
FSC
www.fsc.org
FSC® C016779

A catalogue record for this book is available from the British Library.

Front cover: Ennerdale Water
Title page: Tarn Hows

Ordnance Survey

Pathfinder® Guides — **Britain's best-loved walking guides**